Cyber Security:
The Lost Decade

Why large organisations still
struggle with decade-old security
problems – and how to fix them

Selection of Key Articles

2015–2021

Jean-Christophe Gaillard

In collaboration with
Neil Cordell, Natasha McCabe and Vincent Viers

THE
Security
Transformation
RESEARCH FOUNDATION

JC Gaillard is the Founder and Managing Director of Corix Partners, a London-based Boutique Management Consultancy Firm focused on assisting CIOs and other C-level executives in resolving Cyber Security Strategy, Organisation and Governance challenges.

He is a leading consultant, a senior executive and a global cyber security influencer with over 25 years of experience developed in several financial institutions in the UK and continental Europe, and a track-record at driving fundamental change in the Security field across global organisations, looking beyond the technical horizon into strategy, governance, culture, and the real dynamics of transformation.

French and British national permanently established in the UK since 1993, he holds an Engineering Degree from Telecom Paris and has been co-president of the Cyber Security group of the Telecom Paris alumni association since May 2016.

He runs the Corix Partners blog and the "Security Transformation Leadership" publication on Medium.

He contributes regularly to the Business 2 Community and Business Transformation Network blogs as well as the London Tech Leaders and TechNative websites; he has also posted regularly in the past on The Digital Transformation People, IoTforAll and Experfy platforms.

He is an expert contributor on the CIO Water Cooler, and has previously published articles on InfoSecurity Magazine, Computing, the C-Suite.co.uk, Info Sec Buzz, Disruption Hub, and the IoD Director websites.

He is involved with techUK as part of their Cyber People Series, which explores how CISOs should engage at C-Suite and Board level, with a first report released in December 2020.

He also collaborates with leading analysts firm Kuppinger Cole in Germany, with the Association for Data and Cyber Governance in the US and with the Edutec Alliance in Brazil.

He has been ranking consistently in the top 5 of global influencers with Thinkers360 on cybersecurity.

He animates the Security Transformation Research Foundation, a dedicated think-tank and research body affiliated to Corix Partners, aimed at approaching Security problems differently and producing innovative and challenging research ideas in the Security, Business Protection, Risk and Controls space, and co-produces the weekly Cyber Security Transformation podcast on Anchor.

He is also a Non-Executive Director with Strata Security Solutions and has been a member of the NextWorld Capital European Advisors Network since 2014.

Twitter: @Corix_JC

Neil Cordell > https://www.linkedin.com/in/neilcordell/

Natasha McCabe > https://www.linkedin.com/in/natasha-mccabe/

Vincent Viers > https://www.linkedin.com/in/vincent-viers/

Contents

Foreword

Cyber Security: The Lost Decade

I have been involved with information security matters for over 20 years and started writing regularly on the topic in 2015.

Talking to CISOs, CIO, CEOs and their teams as part of my day-to-day field work as consultant, I was horrified by what I was seeing in too many large corporates in terms of security maturity levels and the actual problems some were still struggling with – something that goes way beyond anecdotal evidence and is at the heart of survey after survey every year.

After all, information security good practices have been well established for over 20 years and many industry bodies have been promoting them and evolving them throughout that period.

Why is it that large firms which have had fully functioning information security teams in place all that time, and have spent – collectively – hundreds of millions on the topic if not more on cyber security, are still struggling today with issues – such as patch management – which should have been on their radar for over 10 years?

There is truly a cyber security lost decade for many between the CodeRed, Slammer and Blaster outbreaks of 2001–2003 and the Wannacry and Not Petya attacks of 2017.

By failing to get the basics right in terms of security during that time while continuing to engage in massive cloud-driven business transformation programmes which have turned the enterprise into a truly borderless hybrid, many large firms have dramatically increased their level of exposure to cyber threats. And now the acceleration of the digital transformation emboldened by the COVID crisis – which has also heightened cyber threats – is making things even more complex. And politicians and regulators are now involved as the GDPR and CCPA have shown us over the past few years, now with privacy legislations building up across the U.S. and worldwide.

At Board level, the "when-not-if" paradigm around cyber-attacks has taken root, but it creates fundamentally different dynamics for CISOs and CIOs, as the focus shifts radically from risk and compliance towards execution and delivery, often in exchange of massive investments around security (at least pre-COVID).

To embed those different dynamics around cyber security and make true progress, large organisations must stop thinking of the topic in pure technological terms, look back and address urgently the underlying cultural and governance issues that have been the true roadblocks of that "lost decade".

This is the theme I have been developing over the past 6 years through my contribution to the Corix Partners blog and we offer you in this book a selection of articles published between February 2015 and August 2021, in collaboration with Neil Cordell, Natasha McCabe and Vincent Viers.

They frame our reflexion on those matters and offer – we think – elements of solution to start changing the narrative around cyber security.

Most articles would have been reposted on Linkedin and syndicated on Medium and other blogs or websites such as "CIO Water Cooler" or "Business 2 Community". I would like to take the opportunity here to thank them for their support.

Overall, many thanks to all – clients, partners, friends – who have been at the heart of this body of work.

I hope readers will find what follows thought-provoking and that it will help some move forward.

JC Gaillard
August 2021

Introduction

#1 Cyber Security is not a risk

24 April 2015 – 13 August 2015 (for the original articles)[1]
10 August 2017 (for the combined article)

Boards must now focus on reality and take genuine action

Describing Cyber Security as a risk is a language oddity that keeps appearing at an alarming rate.

It is a dangerous and simplistic shortcut, typical of the shallow nature of some debate taking place around these issues on social media.

Cyber Security is not a "risk". Cyber Security results from the proper application of proportionate Controls to protect an organisation from the Cyber Threats it faces. Cyber Risk results from the absence or inefficiency of such Controls.

With survey after survey highlighting that large organisations struggle to demonstrate any kind of Cyber Security maturity, the time has come for Boards to approach the problem from the right Management angle and take real action.

Cyber Security can no longer be treated as a balancing act between costs, risk and the need to ensure regulatory compliance anymore.

The Boards of large organisations must focus on ensuring that the necessary Controls are properly implemented across the true geographic perimeter of the enterprise, taking into account without complacency the role of external partners and suppliers.

Technology alone will not help large organisations get out of such a dead-end. They have focused for too long on merely technical and tactical solutions to their Cyber Security challenges, in search of silver bullets that simply don't exist.

---

1 The date after each article indicates when it was first posted either on the Corix Partners blog (http://corixpartners.com/blog) or on Linkedin Pulse. Multiple dates indicate that the article was first posted on Linkedin Pulse then on the Corix Partners blog, or that it was originally published on the Corix Partners blog in multiple parts. Most of the articles in the book were also syndicated at later dates on other blogs such as "Medium", "The Digital Transformation People", "CIO Water Cooler", "Business 2 Community" or "The Innovation Enterprise".

Organisations need to reflect on where the roadblocks are that have prevented them from reaching a satisfactory level of maturity in the face of current threats, in spite of decades of spending in the IT and Information Security space.

They need to rethink and rewire their approach in a way that will enable them to demonstrate a degree of genuine resilience, instead of merely throwing money at the latest technology product.

Boards must focus on ensuring that accountabilities and responsibilities are properly in place to make sure the enterprise remains adequately protected from Cyber Threats.

Cyber Security cannot be the responsibility of "everybody". In most cases, it should fall in the portfolio of the CIO or the COO, and be cascaded down to a CISO who has the management experience, personal gravitas and political acumen to drive change.

Lasting change in that space will be complex and take time. Boards must ensure that a long-term Cyber Security roadmap is in place and stick to it. Changing approach every time an incident happens elsewhere – or every time a new CISO comes in – will simply kill any change momentum. This long-term roadmap must be supported by a Governance Framework that distributes accountabilities and responsibilities from the Board down across the entire enterprise, including IT, HR, Business Units & Geographies.

Time has come for Boards to stop treating Cyber Security as a "Risk" (i.e. something that may or may not happen): This is now a matter of WHEN, not IF. Boards must focus on reality and take genuine Management action to drive the implementation of protective Controls against the genuine Cyber Threats their business is facing. This is not a matter of budget or resources anymore but a very simple matter of priorities – and possibly a matter of survival for some firms.

Technology Alone Will Not Help

#2 Information Security Governance: Building lasting protection against cyber threats

19 February 2015

Defining Governance within the context of Information Security

Governance will always mean different things to different people.

In small organisations, Governance tends to be seen as a mere piece of consultant's jargon. Relationships, politics and decision-making processes are simpler and it is easier to make sure that everyone pulls in the same direction.

But as organisations grow in size and become operationally more complex (often through acquisitions), those aspects become more complex as well. Coherent action becomes less of a natural concept, and making things happen in a coherent manner requires concerted management action.

This is particularly true in the Information Security space because of the inherent cross-silo nature of the actions involved to protect the business. For example, a coherent identity and access management platform requires concerted action across HR, business units and IT – and each of them might have their own agenda and understanding of the problems.

Information Security Governance needs to encompass all the management mechanisms that ensure coherent action across all stakeholders with the view of delivering effective and efficient information protection to the business. It can only stem from a clear Information Security strategic vision and requires all stakeholders to agree on a clear definition of their respective roles and responsibilities.

The term "Governance" has long suffered from a serious lack of comprehension surrounding its meaning, and poor Governance around Information Security has led to many organisations putting themselves at unnecessary levels of cyber risk.

Effective Information Security Governance must involve the proper management of all the activities which an organisation needs to carry out in order to maximise the protection of the information it processes. It should ensure the protection of key information assets from relevant threats through the layered application of the right controls at people, process and technology levels – while managing any element of risk that may result from the absence or inefficiencies of these controls.

The problems with the reactive approach to Information Security

Unfortunately, many large organisations have historically seen and continue to approach Information Security mostly from a compliance angle – essentially managing Information Security issues on an ad-hoc basis, in a reactive manner, in order to satisfy audit and compliance needs. Throwing money at the problem, through vast audit or compliance-driven programmes of work, is often frightfully expensive (in particular for larger firms) and rarely delivers in full across all geographies. While this approach may provide a degree of temporary protection in some areas, it is often financially inefficient – tending to focus on arbitrary controls to tackle arbitrary threats and leaving organisations exposed as a result.

To break this cycle, large organisations need to build a true understanding of the real nature of the threats they face – and the real controls they have in place at people, process and technology levels to protect themselves against those threats. By doing so, many of them will realise that the potential damage that might result from those threats (to operations, finances and reputation) is primarily the result of the absence of (known and implementable) controls at a number of levels. And that effective long-term information protection cannot stem only from reactive or technical one-off solutions.

They will also realise that it is key to bring all the relevant stakeholders on board and drive concerted actions amongst them to fix those problems. To achieve that, large organisations need to build a strategic vision and the right Governance framework around Information Security.

It's often the responsibility of the CIO to ensure that the whole organisation, including board level management, understand the importance and complexity of Information Security challenges – and architect coherent action through the implementation of a medium to long-term Information Security strategy to engineer lasting protection.

But in order to thoroughly address the issue of Information Security on an ongoing basis, Information Security must become part of a mind-set, embedded into the broader Governance and culture of an organisation. For many organisations, this is a true quantum leap in terms of change.

Creating lasting organisational change within the context of Information Security

For large organisations, where the Information Security focus has been for a long time on tactical projects, real change is always a challenging medium to long-term journey. Effective change has its roots firmly planted in corporate Governance and culture, and can take years to achieve.

From directors who may be unconcerned about the Information Security risk the business faces, to IT teams who may view strict Information Security Governance as a barrier to flexibility and their ability to innovate, it's important to break down organisational silos and get all stakeholders working towards a common goal.

An effective Information Security Governance Framework is one essential piece of that jigsaw. It should distribute roles and responsibilities clearly amongst all stakeholders and act as a dampener – keeping things smoothly in motion (aligned with business objectives across the entire organisation), while reducing the risk of rapid and potentially damaging negative tactical reactions to Information Security issues.

It is only by getting key employees on-board with a medium to long-term Information Security vision and giving them clear roles and responsibilities as part of a clear Information Security Governance Framework that you can create a sense of direction and purpose – and it's only through sustaining this over the medium to long-term that true organisational change can occur.

#3 Technology alone cannot transform failing cyber security practices

16 July 2015

The first RSA Cyber Security Poverty Index[1], published in June 2015, measures a number of large organisations against a sample of controls taken out of the US NIST Cyber Security Framework – collecting data from 400 security professionals across 61 countries. The results highlight that 75% of participants show a significant Cyber Security risk exposure. This recent survey is likely to drive discussions at the upcoming 2015 RSA Asia, Pacific & Japan conference due to be held on the 22nd-24th July in Singapore.

The roadmap proposed by RSA to move out of "cyber poverty" involves endorsing the NIST Cyber Security Framework, balancing controls against prevention, monitoring, and resilience (claiming 80% resources are currently focused on prevention) – and finally fixing the disconnect between cyber-policies and operational execution.

RSA qualifies the results of their survey as reflecting an "unacceptable status quo" and concludes by saying that it is time to "start thinking about Security differently and start doing Security differently".

None of this is really new and, in fact, the results strongly echo those of an earlier survey conducted by McKinsey & Co for the 2014 World Economic Forum. We commented on those in an article published on Computing.co.uk in February 2015[2].

There is little to argue in principle about the roadmap suggested by RSA, but large organisations that want to transform their Cyber Security practice and build maturity must look at their current Cyber Security situation – without complacency and before jumping into action.

1 RSA Cyber Security Poverty Index, June 2015

2 How to achieve effective cyber security in a hyperconnected world, February 2015 (https://www.computing.co.uk/ctg/opinion/2396800/how-to-achieve-effective-cyber-security-in-a-hyperconnected-world)

Endorsing the NIST Cyber Security Framework and better balancing resources between prevention, monitoring, and resilience is a good thing to do, but again – it's nothing new. Large organisations must look back and confront the reasons why they have not acted before on matters of Information or Cyber Security.

The NIST Cyber Security Framework in particular follows in a long series of similar approaches that spans the best part of the last 10 to 15 years: "Identify-Protect-Detect-Respond-Recover" sounds a lot like an update to the "Plan-Do-Check-Act" of ISO 27001:2005, itself replicating a concept introduced in BS 7799 back in 2002.

Of course, threats continue to evolve and are now more virulent than ever, but basic controls (in particular around monitoring and resilience) have been well mapped out for a long time. Large organisations, that have been spending large sums on Information Security over the past decade, with fully staffed, fully functioning Information Security functions during this time – should not be in a position of such low maturity today.

Those large organisations (including those in the public sector, where maturity levels seem to be even lower) have to examine where the roadblocks are that have prevented them from making progress in the past – and ensure these are neutralised or removed. In our opinion, this is a problem deeply rooted in governance, organisational and cultural matters – underpinning the disconnect between policy and execution that RSA has rightly diagnosed.

With maturity levels at rock bottom, in spite of decades of Information Security spend, it is indeed time to start thinking about Cyber Security differently. However, it is not a technical revolution that is required – and there is no software, hardware or technical service alone that can make change happen in that space.

Security technology can support the right Security organisation and enable the right Security processes, but a genuine and lasting transformation of Cyber Security approaches can only come from a full rewiring of existing Information Security practices. This must come from the top and will require a long-term transformative vision articulated into a strategic Security Roadmap and a sound Security Governance model reaching across all corporate silos and geographies.

#4 The Misleading Message of the Technology Industry

26 April 2016 – 23 June 2016

True independence is a rare commodity in the Cyber Security world

There is an incredible amount of material online and on social media around cyber security. But the vast majority of it is either sponsored by technology vendors or directly associated with them. They range from start-ups or specialised software houses (large and small), all the way up to industry heavy weights. They sponsor industry events, conferences and publications of all sorts, including the specialised supplements of many broadsheets and magazines. They produce white papers, reports, surveys and the like, in numbers sufficient to fill several bookcases every year.

Broadly speaking, those reports have been saying the same thing for the past few years: Cyber threats are evolving faster than people can react; investments in cyber security are insufficient to keep up; maturity stays at low levels in large corporations and across the public sector; it must now become a "Board-level priority" for things to change.

Some of those aspects match what we observe in the field every day, but the overall message coming from technology vendors is simplistic and has 2 major flaws:

1. It tricks large corporations and the general public in believing that cyber security is something new.

    This is not the case. Cyber threats have not appeared overnight. In fact, they have been evolving for the best part of the last 15 years and therefore there is a vast body of good practice that will go a long way to protect any business.

    But those good practices have to be in place, and often are not. Cutting corners around those on grounds of costs or convenience simply creates opportunities that cyber threats can target. And indeed, many recent breaches seem to relate to the absence of security controls that have been regarded as good practice for years and should have been in place.

The sad reality is that, in spite of decades of spending in the information security space, many large organisations are still struggling today with problems going back to an era where security measures were seen as a necessary evil imposed by regulations – at odds with functionality and preventing innovation and agility.

2. It perpetuates the false idea that the problem is technical in nature.

   In fact, it is increasingly becoming a matter of mindset, culture and governance.

   Many problems are rooted in decades of neglect, badly targeted investment, adverse prioritisation or complacency, and there can be no miracle solution – technical or otherwise – in such situation: Avoiding cyber security breaches, or dealing with them, requires coherent action over time across the whole organisation.

Only by identifying and removing the roadblocks that have prevented progress in the past, will large organisations establish a genuine and lasting transformation dynamic. This is often a complex change process that could take years and require relentless drive to succeed. It is not about deploying yet another piece of security software.

Of course, technology can and does enable some aspects of the cyber security transformation, but it needs to be rooted in a transformative vision that puts people and process first. And embedded within a target operating model that allocates clear roles and responsibilities across the whole enterprise, not just the IT department.

Those messages are rarely heard in the media, which are often dominated by the short-term agenda of tech vendors. And even when they do get mentioned, they are often lost in the midst of a vast amount of technology noise and are hardly audible or credible.

True independence is a rare commodity in the Cyber Security world, but it is essential for large organisations to navigate those waters and develop a genuinely protective practice, instead of simply listening to the latest technology buzz.

#5 Understanding historic roadblocks is key to unlocking the dynamics to digital resilience

23 July 2015

McKinsey & Company, together with most leaders in Strategy Consulting, have involved themselves more and more in Cyber Security over the past few years – and their latest article "Repelling the cyberattackers" [1]offers an excellent analysis and set of actions towards Digital Resilience. Congratulations to James Kaplan, Allen Weinberg and their teams

In fact, the article echoes many themes we have mentioned here repeatedly, in particular throughout our series "The CIO Guide to a successful Information Security Practice" (a summary of which was published here):

Cyber Security is too often seen as a mere technical discipline, while in fact, it is a complex cross-silo activity that has to reach beyond IT into the Business and other corporate practices – such as HR, Legal and Procurement

Cyber Security must be approached as a structured practice, not just a collection of IT projects – and sound Governance is paramount

It is essential to think of Cyber Security from a business process perspective, supported by technology – and not the other way round. The business will always understand controls when spoken to in its own language

In such context, reporting lines, organisational structures and the personal profile of the Cyber Security transformation agents (the CISO and their team is most large organisations) are key to success

The article rightly focuses on driving tangible action, instead of "highly abstract (and therefore largely meaningless)" risk discussions – which is a view we totally endorse.

---

1 McKinsey & Co, « Repelling the Cyberattackers », 2015 (http://www.mckinsey.com/business-functions/digital-mckinsey/our-insights/repelling-the-cyberattackers)

It puts the road to Digital Resilience into some historical perspective, which was one of our criticisms of the 2014 report "Cyber Security in a Hyper connected World" – published ahead of the World Economic Forum meeting in Davos last year[1]. But it must be acknowledged that the journey to Digital Resilience will be specific to each large organisation, and that most are still at fairly low levels of Cyber Security maturity.

In spite of decades of spending in the IT and Information Security space, many large organisations are still struggling with "pre-2007" problems (in reference to Exhibit 1 from the McKinsey article), where Cyber Security is seen as a necessary evil imposed by regulations – at odds with functionality and preventing innovation and agility, instead of a necessary barrier to protect the business from real and active threats.

On their road to Digital Resilience, organisations have to accept first that Controls are essential, but getting to that realisation after 10 to 15 years of complacency, neglect or short-termist "tick-in-the-box" practices will not be simple. And only by identifying and removing the roadblocks that have prevented progress in the past, will they establish a genuine and lasting transformation dynamic.

In our opinion, this is a problem deeply rooted in governance, organisational and cultural matters that requires a fundamental rethinking and rewiring of Information Security practices.

This must come from the top and in that context, Board involvement and "senior cross-functional oversight" is essential – as the article rightly states – to avoid a "mere patchwork of compromises". The Board must be prepared (and able) to look at the problem over the long-term and stick to it.

Of course, real change in that space will require a long-term transformative vision (supported and funded by the Board), articulated into a strategic Security Roadmap and a sound Security Governance model – reaching across all corporate silos and geographies.

---

1 World Economic Forum, 'Risk and Responsibility in a Hyper-connected World', January 2014 (with McKinsey & Co)

But fundamental to success will be the personal gravitas, political acumen and management skills of the key transformation agent (the CISO in most large organisations). The CISO should have the seniority and experience required, and remain in charge over the necessary period to oversee real change – meaning they may have to consider their tenure over a 5 to 7 year horizon in many cases.

In such sensitive area, changing approach every 2 to 3 years, every time a new CISO comes in or every time something happens at Board level, is simply a recipe for failure. And when coupled with an excessive technical focus and short-termist compliance obsession, this could be the main reason why so many large organisations still show such low levels of Cyber Security maturity today.

#6 Cyber Security Skills Gap: What Skills Gap?

2 March 2017

The Cyber Security Industry needs more talent; but at which level and to do what?

Here is a theme that has cyber security experts gripped: There is an enormous problem of skills across the cyber security industry. Not enough professionals. Hundreds of thousands of jobs remaining unfilled. It's a massive challenge and a key to the evolution of the industry. A fundamental factor preventing progress.

But frankly, what is all this about? What are those jobs? What would be their purpose?

You don't have to read much between the lines to see that most of the skills gap message emanates from the incestuous eco-system formed by large consultancies, their clients in large established security teams in large organisations, and the recruitment firms servicing both.

Most of the language used when describing the missing skills is heavily technical in nature and points towards the same IT security space: Pen testers, SOC engineers, threat analysts etc.; as many jobs supporting large tech platforms built on tech products; and behind that, the same – misleading – message from the tech industry, that all this is a just technical problem that can be fixed by buying more tech…

So it becomes apparent pretty quickly that the "cyber skills gap" story dominating the headlines is just another aspect to an old theme: The cyber security industry obsession with finding technical and tactical silver bullets, to a problem that is in too many cases rooted in decades of adverse prioritisation, complacency, a "tick-in-the-box" culture around compliance and – fundamentally – poor corporate governance.

I am not in denial about the threats and I fully appreciate the challenges faced by large global firms and government agencies in dealing with cyber defence, but when talking to CISOs and senior executives in smaller firms, and those truly trying to create a long-term transformational dynamic around cyber security, it is a very different skills gap we hear about.

What they crave is management experience, personal gravitas, political acumen and internal business focus – coupled with strong control-mindedness and a degree of cyber knowledge of course – because this is the true combination that drives change.

Those are attributes that you develop through real field experience. You are not likely to find them in junior consultants or ex-auditors. And few successful IT executives are likely to follow that path, because the whole IT industry is measuring success in terms of delivery, functionality and performance, not in terms of controls or security; and therefore, IT security has never been – and will not be for the short-term – a rewarding path to the top for most IT executives.

So there is indeed a skills gap in the security management space, and a pretty serious one. And this is the real big story around missing cyber skills.

To fix this, you have to make control functions attractive to increase the pool of younger professionals who want to get involved in them, learn and build a career out of it, both within and outside IT.

It requires credible board-level support and engagement, a credible regime of tangible incentives, both in terms of financial rewards and training, and credible role models and career success stories. There may also be a role for business schools to play to start shifting the narrative around cybersecurity leadership.

It can be done in firms – large and small – but it becomes a true matter of corporate culture, and in many cases, a matter of real transformation.

#7 Rethinking and rewiring Information Security

30 June 2015

Information Security is still broadly perceived as an IT discipline built around technical products and projects – you just have to open any industry magazine or publication to see it. The InfoSec Europe exhibition in London in June 2015 would have attracted around 350 vendors and tens of thousands of technologists, and there are several similar shows around the world every year.

The "three lines of defence" models promoted in some form or another by various standards such as COSO or ISO31000 are poorly understood and poorly applied. Information Security is often arbitrarily kept in a technical first line, in spite of its complex nature, requiring a true implementation across the three lines of defence – and across many corporate silos.

In practice, this excessive technical focus, which spans the entire industry history, is failing for most large organisations. In fact, many of these organisations claim to spend in excess of 3% of their total IT spend on cyber security, but in spite of the amounts invested over the years – 79% have not yet achieved an acceptable level of cyber security maturity[1].

In our opinion, this failing situation is rooted in the lack of cultural fit between Security and IT mind-sets; technologists are trained and incentivised to deliver functionality, not controls – and this fundamental mismatch has two critical consequences:

Firstly, it deprives Information Security of the raw talents it deserves. Information Security is rarely seen as a career path to the top – and IT executives with potential look elsewhere for development. As a result, Information Security leaders are often good technologists – but lack the management experience, personal gravitas or political acumen they would need to be truly successful in such a complex role.

---

1 World Economic Forum & McKinsey & Company, 'Risk and Responsibility in a Hyper-connected World', January 2014)

Secondly, it drives adverse prioritisation and focuses Information Security towards ad-hoc tactical point solutions. At best, the CISO becomes a 'fire-fighter', at worse an IT Program Manager amongst many others – or a hobbyist playing around with 'pet projects' and changing jobs every couple of years as soon as the going gets tougher.

This tactical and technical focus rarely delivers true results in large organisations. They have become increasingly dependent on a larger and larger number of third-parties, their Information Security problems are often global and complex in nature, and the threats they face continue to evolve at a faster and faster pace. The geographical, operational and technical complexity of large organisations requires a proper governance framework – that is rarely in place – to enable the true delivery of Information Security solutions on a global scale.

This lack of results can drive middle-management frustration and budgetary tensions around Information Security internally, which in turn brews demotivation and further talent alienation away from InfoSec functions. It is often also the lack of results (or insufficient or slow progress) which attracts the attention of auditors and regulators on these matters; those are often 'low hanging fruits' in absence of any strategic vision around Information Security.

This, in turn, is effective at drawing the attention of Executive Management towards the topic, but for all the wrong reasons. And when coupled with the increasing media and political attention around cyber security, it simply aggravates the tactical dynamics around InfoSec. Driven by endemic fears of negligence claims and short-termist compliance obsessions, money which wasn't there yesterday suddenly appears out of nowhere just to fix audit or compliance issues. Senior executives can go to the media or claim between themselves that "cyber is on our agenda and money is there", but in practice, the lines haven't really moved at all – and the same old mistakes are being perpetuated.

Over time, Information Security becomes an overhead and a problem, instead of a necessary barrier against real and active threats to the business. And in practice, money is often simply wasted to put ticks in boxes. A large number of technology companies make a good living in that space, but this eco-system is inherently un-healthy. This results in stagnating protection levels and low cyber security maturity, which is what the World Economic Forum report highlighted last year.

Organisations which find themselves in such a situation – and want to break these dynamics of failure – must rethink their approach and rewire their Information Security practice by acting at 3 levels:

1. The profile of the CISO needs to be right in order to drive change. Look without complacency at the Information Security history across the firm, and at the barriers that have prevented progress. The CISO needs to have the right amount of management experience, personal gravitas and political acumen to be credible with all stakeholders across corporate silos (not just technologists) – these are attributes of seniority. Information Security is not just a technical discipline. Information exists in physical as well as digital form – and is constantly manipulated by people as part of business processes. It needs to be protected at digital, physical and functional levels. Only with the right attitude and experience will the CISO be able to reach out of IT to all stakeholders and drive success. Of course, the reporting line of the CISO is of paramount importance in that context and we have commented several times about that in earlier articles. It should be to the CIO or the COO in most cases and delegating down must be avoided at all costs, as it would simply confuse objectives, create opportunities for political tensions with stakeholders – and destroy any credibility around the real desire of Executive Management to drive change.

2. The CISO needs to structure their relationship with all stakeholders as part of an Information Security Governance Framework, positioning roles, responsibilities and accountabilities across the Information Security space and across the whole organisation from the top down. The CISO must also define a proper Target Operating Model for the Information Security team itself, which would give it a strong backbone, a clear structure and an un-ambiguous sense of purpose internally. All this is key to driving success. For example, you cannot imagine delivering a successful Identity & Access management programme of work without the

involvement of HR (and the business units if they are allowed to hire & fire directly) – and without clear demarcation lines around what gets done within the InfoSec team and what remains outside of it. The whole Governance model should also address, without complacency, the full geographical spectrum of the business – and its true nature in terms of dependencies on third-parties.

3. The CISO needs to build a long-term Information Security Strategic Roadmap and be prepared to stay in charge for the time it will take to deliver it. Real and long-lasting change in the Information Security space will involve a cultural shift for most large organisations – and the embedding of a structured practice and a controls mind-set in the way the organisation works. It will not happen quickly. It could typically involve an initial transformation cycle of several years, followed by a consolidation cycle of several years. The CISO and key team members may have to consider their tenure over a 5 to 7 year horizon to genuinely drive change through. During the period, all actions (technical or not) must be pinned against a consistent long-term backdrop, including any unavoidable short-term tactical initiatives (typically driven by incidents, audit observations or compliance requirements). Inconsistencies and a constant reshuffling of priorities would simply kill the change momentum, so would the untimely removal of key personnel.

Raising the profile of the CISO (and their reporting line where necessary) will break the dynamics of talent alienation around Information Security. Sound Governance coupled with a better management & political acumen at senior level within InfoSec will break the dynamics of failure around delivery. Pinning success against a long-term backdrop and ensuring that the CISO and key personnel remain in place throughout will help Executive Management develop a true sense of purpose around Information Security, beyond short-termism or audit and compliance obsessions.

Over time, Information Security should become a valuable protective function at the heart of the organisation – not just an IT department that deals with audit issues.

#8 Why are we still facing so many security products and vendors?

23 May 2019

A symptom of the unhealthy relationship between cyber security and large firms

As we reach one of the high points of each year's conference season, one has to reflect once more on the staggering number of products and vendors active across the cybersecurity space.

Once again, they will line up in their hundreds at Infosec in London and elsewhere. Of course, not all of them are making money; many are still burning the cash of their generous VCs, but the fact that such a crowded market still attracts large amounts of investment is still – in itself – bewildering.

In addition, many of those products still aim to address security requirements which are as old as security good practices themselves, for example across segments such as Incident and Event Management or Identity & Access Management.

To see those segments so fragmented across so many players after 15 or 20 years of evolution is not the sign of a healthy marketplace.

They should have consolidated years ago and each should be dominated by a few players – in addition to the usual big names – all bound by healthy competition.

The fact that it's not the case simply tell us that buyers are not serious: They do not buy those products because they address a real business need: They only buy those products to put ticks in compliance boxes, to close down some audit points or in support of somebody's pet project. Or very often, in reactive mode, under pressure to show responsiveness after an incident and without any attempt – or time – to analyse the market, compare offerings and structure a defensive strategy.

Even if the "tick-in-the-box" market is huge – and GDPR has just made it bigger – in the long-term, nobody wins at that game: Product development ends up driven by regressive compliance-led dynamics, instead of positive dynamics aimed at countering ever-evolving threats, poorly-protected buyers get breached and the industry at large stagnates.

In many large organisations, the situation has reached astounding levels: The 2019 Cisco CISO benchmark study highlights that 37% of respondents have more than 10 security vendors to manage (3% have more than 50 !!!)

"Best-of-breed" may be an interesting concept in the security space, but as we pointed out above, it is rarely the real reason behind product proliferation, and in practice, it presents operational teams with considerable challenges: How to orchestrate an efficient incident response when the data you need is scattered across so many platforms? How to build an effective and meaningful reporting capability?

And the situation is often compounded by the fact that many security tools only end up partially deployed, or simply covering a fraction of the estate – functionally or geographically.

Firms which find themselves in that mess must stop buying more tech, look back at their genuine security requirements in relation to the threats they face and start building a consolidation strategy.

They should also look beyond the products marketplace and consider the ever-growing services offerings in that space. MSSPs have been active for over 15 years but the cloud has also facilitated the emergence of a number of new players in recent years.

Consolidation and integration become key factors, as the "when-not-if" paradigm around cyber attacks takes centre-stage with senior executives and their focus shifts away from risk and compliance, towards execution and delivery.

All those who have been riding the compliance wave should bear that in mind.

#9 Cyber Security:
The Operational Illusion

21 January 2021

Security culture and governance eat tech for breakfast

Looking back at what happened at ground level throughout the COVID crisis, it is clear that the focus has been entirely on operational matters: From moving into remote working at scale for the services industry, to keeping supply chains working for the manufacturing sector, or many retail firms having to re-invent themselves as digital businesses, literally within weeks. It has all been about keeping the lights on, understandably.

Tech and cyber security have been – and still are – at the heart of all this, and, as we wrote back in April 2020, it is hard not to see those sectors coming out as winners once the dust has settled over the pandemic.

But for now, the focus has been entirely tactical; nobody can see beyond the short term, and it is likely to remain the case for the best part of 2021. This is hard to criticize as a business approach given the scale and depth of the crisis, but in many firms, when it comes to cyber security, it is simply perpetuating and aggravating an endemic tendency, which over the past 10 years, has kept CISOs trapped in endless firefighting, has prevented them from developing in terms of leadership and management skills, and has not brought forward the necessary maturity changes around security in terms of governance, organization and culture.

This will be a serious problem in many firms which would have been locked for years in slow-moving and expensive security programmes, and now need to transform their security practices at pace as cyber security has become a pillar of their "new normal".

It is an illusion to think that all the tactical and operational focus which has been prevailing around cyber security since the start of the pandemic, is transformative.

It might be counter-intuitive but moving past this operational obsession with cyber security is key, as we look ahead, to unlock long-term transformational dynamics.

The idea that the consistent protection of the business from cyber threats can result entirely and purely from the implementation of technical tools – or ad-hoc pen tests for that matter ... – is fundamentally flawed, in absence of a coherent overarching vision.

Tactical knee-jerk reactions simply add layer upon layer of technical legacy. Over time, the poor delivery of poorly selected tools breeds distrust with senior management, who can't help but seeing that breaches continue to happen in spite of the millions spent. The inefficient reverse-engineering of security processes around the capabilities of the tools leads to escalating operational costs, staff shortages and apparent skills gaps. CISOs feel alienated and leave. All this builds a narrative by which security becomes a cost and a problem, and overtime nobody wins.

Throwing money at the problem – for the industries where that is still an option in the midst of the COVID crisis – is not the answer for firms where security maturity has stagnated as a result from decades of under-investment and adverse prioritisation by the business.

More than ever, now is the time to think in terms of People first, then, Process THEN Technology, if the objective is to build a lasting transformational dynamic around cyber security.

It is a vision that has to come from the top and be relayed across all the silos of the enterprise. Cyber security cannot be seen as the responsibility of the CIO or the CISO. It needs to be visible and credible as part of a coherent business purpose, communicated coherently to the staff by senior management, and relayed – and enforced – by a proper governance framework.

It is the embedding of security values in corporate culture and corporate governance that should drive the transformative efforts around cyber security and will lead ultimately to effective cyber resilience.

This is certainly harder to put in place than buying more tech or doing one more pen test, but it is the key to long term transformative success around cyber security, in particular as younger generations become more and more sensitive to clarity of purpose and positive business values.

Organising
for Success

#10 The Reporting Line of the CISO is Key to Success

16 April 2015

Why is the reporting line of the CISO still a hot topic amongst Security communities?

The actual role of the CISO varies greatly from one organisation to another – even if, on paper, job descriptions often look similar.

Of course, the best reporting line for the CISO is the one that positions the role in the best way within the organisation – in relation to the real challenges that the CISO is expected to resolve.

But in practice, corporate governance across large organisations also varies greatly, depending of industry sectors and geographical dispersion. Many large organisations operate (efficiently or not) matrix organisations – and, in those cases, it's unlikely that the CISO will have a single reporting line, leading to a large number of variations where formal and informal authority have to be combined. This is well analysed by Peter Berlich in a recent post[1].

Annual surveys published by the Big 4 consultancy firms over the past 10 years have been highlighting such diversity, and show that the reporting lines now span almost the entire spectrum of board members (including the CEO, COO, CAO, CFO, CRO and Legal counsel). Results indicate that a reporting line to the CIO seems to be the most common in the field, however, this still only accounts for approximately one third of the responses to the surveys on average (with all caveats due to the fact that the methodologies vary from one firm to another and respondents could be different from one year to the next).

Reporting lines into IT departments (at levels below the CIO) remain common in many industries, for example accounting for up to 26% of respondents in the Life Sciences sector according to the EY 2014

---

1 Peter Berlich, "For Security, Organizational Structure May be Overrated », February 2015 (https://www.infosecurity-magazine.com/blogs/organizational-structure-overrated/)

Global Information Security Survey[1]. Reporting lines into audit and compliance departments are still commonplace today.

In addition, many of these job titles – in particular, the COO, CAO, CRO and CIO – could hide a variety of actual roles and individual profiles. This is particularly true in larger firms, where multiple reporting and "dotted lines" can also lead to situations where accountability is seen as a vague and relative concept.

In short, the current situation seems to reflect the confusion that has been surrounding Information Security Strategy and Governance for the past 10 to 15 years. Beyond the natural diversity of the CISO roles in terms of content, it seems that many large organisations have treated the CISO reporting line in a casual and ambiguous manner, instead of positioning it in the best way to protect themselves against the genuine threats they're facing.

How important is the reporting line of the CISO?

The reporting line of the CISO is the most essential channel of authority, as it presents to all stakeholders – in an un-equivocal manner – the real level of importance placed on Information Security by the organisation.

Because Information Security is a matter that cuts across too many corporate silos (HR, Legal, Business Units and IT etc.), matrix reporting and "dotted lines" should be avoided. These multiple reporting lines are rarely efficient, rarely understood fully and generally add to the confusion. This can hinder the leadership of the CISO and their ability to deliver.

It is key to go back to basic organisational principles. Ideally, the CISO should have a single reporting line – positioned at a level in the organisation that will maximise the impact of the role. The profile of the CISO should be adequate and suited to a Board-level reporting line and the CISO should have the gravitas, credibility and management experience to influence their peers (as discussed in our February 2015 feature on the C-Suite blog). If the Board feels that's not the case, the Board should start by addressing this issue.

---

1 Ernst & Young, Life Sciences Global Information Security Survey, 2014

If the CISO is expected to get things done across the organisation, the reporting line should be to the CIO or the COO – as these executives are most likely to be the closest to Information Security matters within an organisation.

But ultimately, the actual reporting line decision should be made at Board level – and based on the results of a high level assessment of the maturity of security controls across the organisation.

From that point, the Board should be able to focus on inspiring the right spirit for the role – and there are, broadly speaking, three different types of profiles the CISO can fall under:

The CISO as a Figurehead

The Board may feel that the business is well-protected against Information threats and that the CISO needs to be a "figurehead" – a well-networked senior executive, credible with business leaders and capable of representing the firm at conferences and global events. A reporting line to the CEO or another board member (possibly the COO) may be suitable, particularly for industry sectors or smaller firms where controls are already a mindset.

The CISO as a Firefighter

If the Board is primarily driven by short-termist views and concerned only with the resolution of recurring audit or compliance matters, its priorities will almost always drive a tactical agenda. The CISO will end up in a complex programme manager role, constantly having to influence stakeholders and act as a "firefighter" to keep projects on track – ensuring priorities remain set as they should be across IT and the business.

A reporting line to the CIO or the COO is essential in such context, given the complexity of the CISO role and the cross-silo nature of Information Security challenges. Delegating down must be avoided at all costs, simply because it sends a highly dangerous message across the organisation. Irrespective of the personal profile of the CISO, downward delegation implies that Information Security is not that important and can only fuel internal politics and confuse prioritisation amongst stakeholders.

But this alone is not sufficient enough to ensure success, and the actual success of the CISO will rely entirely on having a proper Information Security Governance Framework in place to ensure that all stakeholders have a clear understanding of their respective roles and responsibilities in the programme delivery, and the way C-level management will be involved.

Most tactical approaches in the Information Security space fail simply because they compromise too much on the last two points.

The CISO as a Change Agent

If the Board is concerned about the maturity level of controls and wants to drive lasting improvements across the organisation, the CISO needs to be a "change agent". It's in this situation that the positioning of the reporting line is most critical.

The reporting line must be given, without exception, to a control-minded senior executive that the Board trusts to supervise change in the Information Security space. Again, this should ideally be the CIO or the COO – and delegating down must still be avoided at all costs, as this is one of the most common failure factors.

Where controls maturity issues are serious enough – particularly in large organisations with a high Internet footprint facing serious cyber security challenges that may bring the whole business down – the CEO must consider whether the situation has reached a critical point. Here, a direct involvement in the resolution of these issues is required and the CEO must consider taking the CISO role as a direct report as a result.

In other situations, where controls maturity is low, it's the need to drive improvement that should be a key factor in the reporting line decision – not arbitrary separation of duties considerations. Separation of duties considerations are often negative organisational devices aimed at dealing with conflicts of priorities generated by non-control-minded executives. In large organisations, these considerations can create more problems than they solve, by engineering arbitrary political barriers with the potential to damage the CISO's leadership ability and hinder change delivery. Internal politics often make it extremely hard to influence change "across the fence" (i.e. in parts of the organisations where you don't belong).

It is key to look at the problem from a positive angle and only give the CISO reporting line to a control-minded senior executive who can be trusted by the Board on their prioritisation, because the key issues are in their area of accountability.

How to determine the best reporting line for the CISO?

The prime focus should be on delivering results, based on a thorough examination of the prime operational focus of the organisation (People/Process/Technology) and its dependency on information attributes (Confidentiality/Integrity/Availability). The CISO reporting line should be positioned in the area where the most change is required and where most of the efforts will be targeted.

Fig. 1: The CISO Reporting Line: Decision Matrix

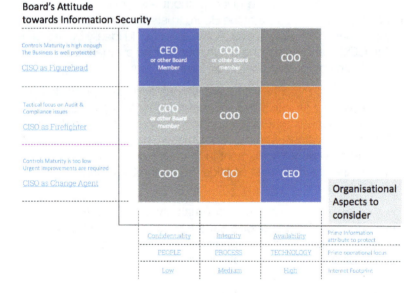

If most of the problems are in IT, the reporting line of the CISO should be to the CIO. If most of the problems are outside IT, the reporting line of the CISO should be to the COO.

Multiple lines of defence and separation of duties considerations must come second to, or be wrapped around, the need to drive results – in particular where Information Security maturity levels are low. Those can be left for the CIO or the COO to drive, as mentioned in our February 2015 feature on the C-Suite blog[1].

If these individuals are not control-minded or the Board feels they cannot be trusted with a Security change programme (or if these individuals simply think they're too busy to take on the role), the Board should ask itself whether it is the attitude that the CIO or COO shows towards Security and controls which is the root cause of the low maturity situation the Board is aiming to resolve.

1 « Information Security: Three Governance Challenges for the CIO This Year » (http://www.thecsuite.co.uk/CIO/index.php/security/210-governance-challenges-for-cio-4435435)

#11 The role of the CISO, the CIO and the Board

22–29 October 2015

Digital Transformation vs. Organisational Legacy

The hybrid role of the CISO

The lines are shifting for the CISO and the CIO.

Beyond the functional distinctions we analysed in our reporting line article (CISO as a Figurehead / CISO as a Fire Fighter / CISO as a Change Agent), we need to consider the positioning of the role in the "three lines of defence" model in more depth.

Our analysis of the best reporting lines for the CISO can be read and would function well in a first or second line positioning for the role. We have expanded upon this in a separate article, focused on GRC and making it work for InfoSec, in which we highlighted a functional model for Information Security to be effective and efficient in a proper second line position.

However, these reflections assumed a reasonably pure application of the concepts and a clear and traditional demarcation between first and second lines. In practice, this is rarely the case. The "three lines of defence" model is often poorly understood and poorly applied, leading to a variety of (more or less dysfunctional) hybrid models.

Judging by social media and broader online engagements, most people holding a CISO job title seem to be in a first line position, in charge of delivering technical protective measures across the IT estate. They have a strong interest in technical security matters, breaches and products.

But the reality is that the role of the CISO has been evolving organically and tactically for many years.

Many CISOs have been forced to develop risk management and compliance reporting capabilities, which should normally sit in second line. This is often driven by the immaturity, irrelevance or lack of interest of the corporate Risk and Compliance functions around them. In a number of cases, this move was prompted or encouraged by auditors or regulators. This is common in many financial firms where Risk and Compliance have been well established corporate practices for decades, but have only just woken up to Information and Cyber risk fairly recently – and are often struggling to articulate a meaningful message in that space.

In a different type of hybrid scenario, some of the few CISOs who seem to be positioned in the second line might have been forced to take on board "first line" operational duties because they were seen as the most able to deliver those successfully.

At the same time, the CISO is almost always a technologist by background – but not always a successful one. We have highlighted many times in previous articles that IT professionals are trained and incentivised to deliver functionality, not controls – and as a result, IT Security is rarely a path to the top.

Information Risk and Compliance practices developed by first line CISOs in a "bottom-up" manner are rarely comprehensive, and often poorly connected to other Risk and Compliance activities taking place across the organisation. Operational activities delivered by second line CISOs are often seen as inefficient and expensive, as many service management activities and technology platforms are often duplicated.

This is generally a symptom of broader governance problems and it is not rare to encounter large organisations where various overlapping functions, such as Information Security, Data Management and Data Protection, co-exist under different reporting lines – with little coherent coordination between them.

This is an environment where many CISOs struggle, burdened with a legacy position and legacy organisational arrangements which do not suit the needs of today's enterprise.

The changing role of the CIO

Most surveys indicate that a majority of CISOs report to the CIO. We have stated repeatedly that it is not necessarily a problem, and that the reporting line should be determined on the basis of functional objectives instead of being driven by arbitrary separation of duties considerations. Those often create unnecessary barriers, fuel internal politics and prevent progress.

At the same time, the role of the CIO has changed and will continue to evolve over the short to mid-term. This is simply driven by the fast-paced evolution of technology over the past 10 years:

Cloud computing has dramatically changed the way IT is structured, delivered and supported. At the coalface, a CTO (Chief Technology Officer) is often in charge of all IT infrastructure aspects, working closely with a large array of external vendors while still dealing with all legacy systems and their problems

Many CIOs must respond to digital transformation challenges and data monetisation opportunities, but they may have to compete with two different types of CDO (Chief Digital/Data Officer) in translating business needs into IT requirements and delivering them. The Chief Digital Officer typically helps the business embrace digital innovation and stay ahead of competition – and often, the Chief Data Officer is charged with helping the business make the most of the data it uses, monetising it where possible using Big Data technology

In parallel to these changes, IT commoditisation at large has introduced layers of "shadow IT" across the enterprise that have to be managed

All of these factors considerably alter the background against which technology solutions have to be conceived and delivered

The CIO has to learn to deal with new stakeholders internally and externally and needs to become more of an influencer and less of a technologist. The CIO also has to learn to be less "in control" of IT and needs to develop a more structured attitude towards risk, in particular with regards to third-parties.

Large organisations are not all at the same degree of maturity in relation to these concepts, but failure to grasp the depth of such transformational challenges may confine the CIO to the management of legacy IT while the CDO role takes centre stage.

New Directions

A structured InfoSec practice can be a key ally for the CIO, but the Board must reward protection to attract and retain talent.

Organising Information Security for a changing IT world

In such context, a strong Information Security practice can be a key asset for the CIO. However, a strong practice must have a clear sense of purpose and a visible backbone upon which the CIO can rely to keep a grip on a changing IT world.

In practice, the CIO must not allow separation to be blurred between first and second lines, and should structure the organisation accordingly.

Enforcing a degree of separation between risk management and controls enforcement within the CIO's organisation could lead to the emergence of 3 distinct functional activities:

• An "Information Risk Management" function, aggregating all traditional second line activities across that space

• An "IT Security" function, focused on the architecture of functional and technical controls (essentially designing IT Security measures and working with all IT stakeholders in that respect, both internally and externally)

• A "Security Operations" function, focused on driving the implementation of controls through the application of technical standards and procedures (these should be designed jointly with the "IT Security" function, based on policies set out by the "Information Risk Management" function and under their validation). The "Security Operations" function (externalised or not) could take a direct role in the delivery of some of these – in particular in the Security Monitoring or Identity Management spaces – and should deal with associated events and incidents

The "Information Risk Management" function should report to the CIO and interface with all non-IT stakeholders, internally and externally, as necessary (Risk, Compliance, internal and external Audit, regulators, etc). The other two functions could be structured at a CIO-1 level (possibly under the CTO or the Head of IT Infrastructure, where such roles exist) and would interface with all IT stakeholders as required.

Fig. 2: Distribution of Information Security Roles against a PDCA cycle

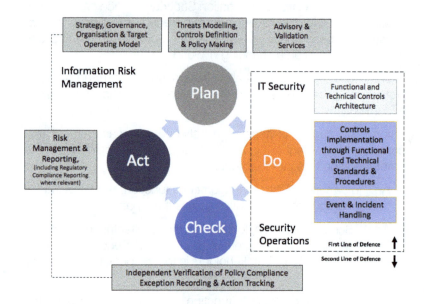

What happens to the CISO tag in such context? It continues to imply a degree of seniority in the role and, if kept in this type of model, should be applied to the "Information Risk Management" function – which is the most complex from a corporate perspective, and has the broader managerial remit.

This is leading us to suggest an alternative organisational model for large corporates to structure InfoSec in the portfolio of the CIO – updating the previous model published in April 2015[1] (itself the result of earlier research work, going back to 2012).

1   Corix Partners blog; "Organising Infosec for Success", April 2015 (http://www.corixpartners.com/organising-infosec-for-success-blog/)

Fig. 3: Organisational Model for Large Firms

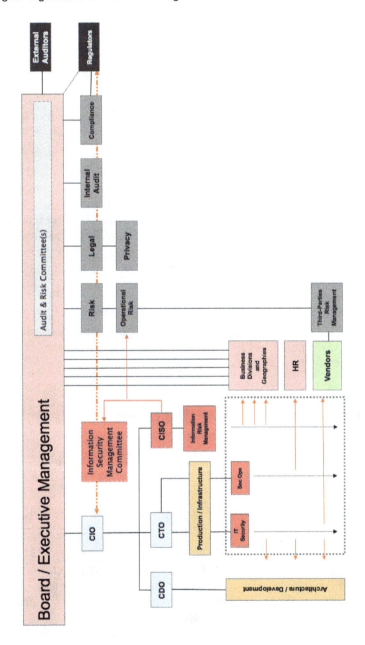

Moving towards the type of model highlighted here could imply splitting legacy CISO roles, and developing a different and more structured target operating model around Information Security.
It would, invariably, involve some form of redistribution of personnel, and skill sets may have to be reviewed and adjusted. In some cases, it may highlight a critical need to invest more in resources to cover areas where little had been done up to now.

The CIO and the Board should consider this a major step towards building a resilient IT practice in the face of virulent cyber threats – rather than continuing to pour resources, on an ad-hoc basis, into arbitrary technical projects.

The argument that this type of model could lead to a "conflict of interests" for the CIO needs to be handled with common sense (in particular in large organisations) and it is key to look beyond simplistic positions. A sound and comprehensive operating model is key to driving change, if that's what is required around Information Security. Arbitrary separations often fuel internal politics and can create unnecessary conflicts.

Boards must incentivise CIOs on cyber security

In past articles, we have queried the control-mindedness of CIOs and implied that it was a major prerequisite for the Board to consider placing Information Security in the CIO's portfolio.

The events of the past few years and the emergence of unprecedented media and political interest around cyber security, as a result of major cyber breaches, make it hard to imagine that any CIO in any large organisation would not take such threats seriously.

Beyond the control-mindedness of the CIO, what matters most today is the way the CIO addresses cyber security priorities – and this is something on which the Board can have a direct influence.

The Board should take an active interest in cyber security matters and drive real action in that space, but it can only work in real life if it translates into real incentives for real people.

CIOs have always been incentivised on cost control and the timely delivery of functionality. It is time for the Board to incentivise CIOs also on the delivery of security controls and the actual protection of the organisation from cyber threats.

These incentives should cascade down to attract and retain talent. Only attracting talent, retaining it over the right timeframes, and applying it at the right level across a structured InfoSec organisation will drive more comprehensive and structured protective operating models – and disrupt the mediocrity dynamics around Information Security, to create the conditions of a true security transformation.

#12 The CISO and the Business

15 June 2017

Keep appointing pure technologists in CISO roles and you'll never win

The Wannacry ransomware attack that affected so many large firms in May 2017 led to a number of animated discussions amongst InfoSec communities.

The corrective patch (fixing the vulnerability targeted by the malware) was out since March for supported systems and many firms were badly hit because of their reliance on the unsupported Windows XP (which reached end of life in 2014).

The timely deployment of security patches has been regarded as a fundamental security good practice since the CodeRed, Slammer and Blaster virus outbreaks over 10 years ago, so how can it be that so many large firms are still struggling with this today?

It cannot be just a matter of security investment: Many of the firms reportedly affected by the outbreak would have had fully functioning security practices all that time and would have been spending millions every year on security products.

It has to be a plain matter of adverse prioritisation of security issues by IT and business leaders.

Which brings under the spotlights the role and profile of the CISO in those firms. Surely it would have been the CISO's job to ensure that those matters remain on the agenda of the right leaders, to communicate their urgency, to drive remedial programmes, and to keep hammering at it until it gets fixed.

What is the security community doing wrong, if it is collectively unable to address a technical issue such as the timely deployment of security patches, over a period of time spanning more than a decade?

One reason that is often put forward by security technologists refers to a language disconnect between the CISO and the Business. Somehow, CISOs are not being heard by business leaders and would need to learn to "speak the language of the business". Such assertion – in itself – raises concerns about the actual profile of the CISO if there are question marks over their ability to rise above mere technological arguments and present them in a language a non-specialist would understand.

Of course, many CISOs are technologists by background; and frankly, security has rarely been seen as a pathway to the top in IT circles, so very often the CISO is either in that job because of a personal interest in the technical aspects of the topic… or because there was little else for them to do.

To break the spiral that has led to the past "lost decade" on cyber security matters, you urgently need to inject talent into the security industry.

It is primarily managerial excellence that is missing and it will have to be attracted by rewarding the right skills at the right level. It is also a matter of cultural transformation for many firms, because it is about changing the value scale on which security is being judged.

To attract the best leaders, Security – i.e. the protection of a firm's assets – has to be seen from the Board down as something fundamental that the firm values and rewards. Not as something you can compromise on to maximise profits, or imposed upon you arbitrarily by regulators.

And if you want your CISO to "talk the language of the business", you could start by appointing someone from the business!!!… or at least an IT leader who is not a mere technology hobbyist and has a true transversal view of your business.

A lot of this is about context:

If you present the patch deployment issue as an IT issue, you will be heard by your business in an IT context and prioritised against other IT topics.

If you present it as a matter of fundamental protection against real and active threats, you will be engaging at a different level. But as a CISO, you will need the right voice, the right gravitas, the right profile in the firm to be heard. This is not only a rational argument. You'll have to use every fact you can find, and always focus your communication with other business leaders on those facts and on the reality of the threats. You'll have to pick your battles and strike at the right time to convince the right people. You'll have to break the "bias of imaginability" – theorised by Kahneman[1] – and it will take time. This is a very serious management role that requires a truly senior profile and a considerable amount of experience. And the willingness to stay on for the right course, and that could be considerably more than a mere couple of years.

Keep appointing pure technologists in CISO roles and you'll never win. The protection of the information the firm needs to function is not a mere technology matter, contrary to what many tech vendors would like you to believe. It has a profound cultural dimension that is at the heart of the relationship between the firm and its employees: You protect naturally what you care about. If your CISO embodies that relation, everything they do will carry that weight and you'll move forward.

---

1   see, for example, Daniel Kahneman, « Thinking, Fast and Slow », 2011

#13 What role for the Group CISO?

27 July 2017

The role of the CISO and their reporting line seems to be a continuing topic of discussion amongst cyber security professionals.

The same title often hides a large diversity of roles, positioned differently across their respective organisations. It often reflects the maturity of each firm towards the appreciation of the threats it faces, the need for business protection, and its appetite for controls.

For large groups, in particular where business units or geographies manage their own bottom line and have a significant degree of autonomy in real terms, it can result in a large population of security practitioners across the group with very diverse approaches, objectives and priorities.

Something that is increasingly a major source of concern in a world that is more and more "hyper connected" and where data is the real "fuel" the business needs to burn on its journey towards digital transformation.

Often at the top is a Group CISO, but what could be their role in such context? And how to make it work?

Of course, security governance at group level cannot exist on its own, and somehow can only work if it follows broadly – and is embedded within – the governance model of the whole group.

As a result, the Group CISO will have to position their role based on 2 broad dimensions:

1. A sound appreciation of the real nature of the governance model at group level:

   Some large groups operate very efficiently in a centralised model, driven by "command-and-control" principles, in which business units and geographies have a limited degree of real autonomy.

   At the other end of the spectrum, and often in different industries, some large groups operate by influence in a very decentralised way, where business units and geographies have a large degree of real autonomy.

In between, a number of – more or less – dysfunctional models are quite common, many inspired by a strong distrust from Head Office and fuelled by internal politics and individual interests.

2. A sound appreciation of the real need for group-wide business interaction:

Again, large groups are very diverse on these aspects. Many would have grown by acquisition over time in a more or less structured manner, and those different acquisitions might be at different degree of integration.

It could be that historically the different parts of the group have always had little in common and therefore little interest in exchanging information or needs to integrate IT systems to operate.

Equally, it could be that the digital transformation is introducing the need for stronger cooperation across the group, as it opens up considerable competitive opportunities for cross-selling which could bring enormous growth (or indeed leave the group behind for ever if they are missed, as competitors sail past).

Understanding these nuances is key for the Group CISO when positioning their role and its key objectives. They will be instinctive to a senior executive who might have spent years or decades in the organisation, but it could be much harder for a newcomer and could take time to grasp.

It is nevertheless a key step and it leads to 3 broad patterns in terms of role for the Group CISO, which we have already identified and analysed in earlier articles, focused on organisation and reporting lines:

The Group CISO as a Figure Head

This is typical of large organisations where diversity is high and leaders lead primarily by influence. The prime objective of the Group CISO should be to communicate and drive a common degree of understanding and awareness amongst all stakeholder's communities. There may also be an element of external representation to the role, within industry bodies, academia or similar groups.

Fig. 4: The Three Main Roles of the Group CISO

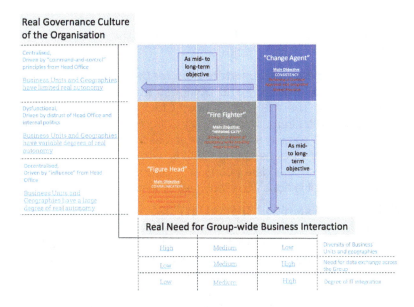

Real Governance Culture of the Organisation

Centralised,
Driven by "command-and-control" principles from Head Office

Business Units and Geographies have limited real autonomy

Dysfunctional,
Driven by distrust of Head Office and internal politics

Business Units and Geographies have variable degrees of real autonomy

Decentralised,
Driven by "influence" from Head Office

Business Units and Geographies have a large degree of real autonomy

As mid- to long-term objective

"Change Agent"
Main Objective:
CONSISTENCY

"Fire Fighter"
Main Objective:
"HERDING CATS"

As mid- to long-term objective

"Figure Head"
Main Objective:
COMMUNICATION

Real Need for Group-wide Business Interaction

High	Medium	Low	Diversity of Business Units and geographies
Low	Medium	High	Need for data exchange across the Group
Low	Medium	High	Degree of IT integration

The Group CISO as a Fire Fighter

This is typical of dysfunctional governance situations, and the prime objective of the Group CISO should be to drive – as much as possible – towards a degree of consistency in security practices across the group, while avoiding major breaches. This is by far the most complex role profile, and it will feel like "herding cats" most of the time for the Group CISO.

The Group CISO as a Change Agent

This is typical of situations where diversity is low and integration is high, with a strong "command-and-control" culture, but where security has never had a high degree of priority. The prime objective of the Group CISO should be to drive for consistency and the delivery of a common approach to security across the group, including shared integrated practices (such as a SOC for instance) where necessary.

How to drive action in all cases: Building a sense of community

In all cases, driving action, creating a sense of value around the Group CISO role and avoiding the "Ivory Tower" syndrome, will involve a number of key principles:

1. **Create a clear mission statement for the Group CISO role, aimed at all security and business stakeholders across the group:** The role of the Group CISO cannot be vague, or difficult to read from the bottom up, or from the top down. But in particular, all security stakeholders across the group must have a clear idea of who the Group CISO is, what they do and why – even if the mandate coming top-down from executive management is not always that clear at their level.

2. **Lead by listening:** The Group CISO function must bring something tangible to the various security stakeholders across the group. It is key to listen to them upfront to understand their constraints and their expectations. Ignoring those would kill trust and emphasize the idea of a Head Office "Ivory Tower" function. This is the most important part and often the hardest, as objectives, maturities and priorities across the group could vary enormously.

3. **In return, build a clear plan with realistic expectations of delivery for all** (at the level at which the group governance model allows you to work with realistic expectations of delivery): It is key to have a clear security plan of action at group level, in which each and every security stakeholder across the group fits and has a role to play with something clear and achievable for them to deliver. They need to have a sense of purpose and feel that collectively they achieve something for the group. This sense of community is the real key to success. In return, the Group CISO should leverage their influence at group level to bring common resources and common budgets to the table that can help achieve common objectives and deliver work on common projects.

4. **Bring all security stakeholders together at least once a year to keep contact, build trust and leverage on their skills and knowledge:** It could be an annual general event where they all come to report on progress and share achievements and issues. It could be several events per year with stronger thematics. In all cases, it is key to reinforce periodically a strong sense of community that transcends what may be happening around the security stakeholders in terms of management, governance or politics at their level, in their region, business unit or subsidiary. It is likely that many will find value in those exchanges, if anything at human level, but also in terms of personal development and technical benchmarking. It can be sometimes a lonely role to be the CISO for a small division or a small region within a large group.

Across all those matters, the reporting line of the Group CISO will be important. As we pointed out above, the different role types overlap those identified in earlier articles: It should be at board-level and dictated by overall objectives for the role. But it's only one aspect.

The personal profile of the Group CISO is essential: Many elements highlighted above call for a degree of seniority, gravitas and political acumen, as well as human qualities to listen to potentially very diverse people and bring them together.

Time is also a key factor as it could take 5 to 10 years to build a genuine security practice at group level in large firms, where nothing existed before. The Group CISO has to be prepared and rewarded to stay the course, and executive management above him has to be capable of working on mid to long-term objectives without deviating every time something happens internally or externally. Knee-jerk reactions on these matters just kill momentum and trust.

Success for the Group CISO role will come from working on all those fronts.

#14 The Current Role of most CISOs Lacks Clarity and Needs to Change

8 March 2016 – 28 April 2016 [with Vincent Viers]

Cyber threats are a growing concern for most organisations. However, it appears that reactive, expensive and inefficient practices are still underpinning most InfoSec strategies. As we have argued in previous articles, it is an issue that must be addressed primarily at the people and process levels through an effective cyber security governance framework – instead of traditional approaches that have historically treated the problem as a mere IT problem and focused only on technology solutions.

The three key pieces of this model are the CISO, the CIO and the Board, whose roles in protecting the organisation against cyber threats must be clearly outlined and commonly understood. However, each of those is currently facing its own challenges in terms of maturity.

In spite of the function having been in existence for decades, the CISO's role and mission still lack clarity and consistency in many large organisations. As a result, the formal distinction between the first and second line of defence in the traditional "three-lines of defence model" is often blurred, and the whole model is generally poorly applied.

The structural pressure that the emergence of Shadow IT and Cloud Computing are exercising on the IT environment of all organisations is forcing an inevitable and ongoing shift in the role of CIOs. They must aim for more cooperation and influence with both internal and external stakeholders and are forced to focus less on the purely technological aspects of the role.

The Board – often scared by recent data breaches – is in the process of becoming fully aware of the cyber security challenges that its organisation is faced with, and its behaviour with regard to InfoSec governance must reflect that acknowledgement. The Board must be consistent in its expectations and explicitly incentivise key senior executives on cyber protection, and not just on product delivery, revenue generation or cost cutting. The reporting line of the CISO, in particular, must unambiguously lie at Board level in order to reflect the importance and the consideration that should be given to this crucial role. The reporting line should be determined on the basis of the challenges the role is facing. Arbitrary separations of duty considerations must be avoided at all costs as they simply fuel internal politics and inefficiencies, and in practice often hinder the implementation of much needed changes.

In such context, the time has come to deconstruct and re-forge the former legacy role of the CISO. Three distinct functions can be identified that would allow the lines between risk management and controls enforcement tasks to be drawn more clearly around traditional PDCA principles.

This new operating model would benefit the CIO by providing them with a stronger and more efficient cyber governance framework. The CISO would also gain in seniority and consideration in the process and could become a key ally to the CIO around digital transformation challenges.

#15 The tenure of the CISO is key to driving security transformation

26 April 2018

Nothing will change until the profile of the CISO is raised and they start to see their role over the mid to long-term

Surveys suggest that the average tenure in a CISO position is around 2 years[11].

Although it seems to vary depending on industry sectors, it is supported by vast amounts of anecdotal evidence and it matches our field experience working with clients. The same goes for the reasons behind the early departures of many CISOs: It often starts with the sense that the internal situation is vastly different from what they had been "sold" throughout the recruitment process; they don't feel valued or listened to; they feel trapped in management models where many key decisions are made elsewhere without their involvement; they feel like they haven't got adequate resources in terms of budget or staff to do what they would like to do. So they leave. Having achieved very little in practice. And in a number of cases, they leave for larger organisations or a larger pay package because of tensions on the recruitment market around those roles.

Then, at best a caretaker manager is appointed; or worse, the role is left vacant for months until a recruitment is made internally or externally. Then someone new comes in, almost always with different views compared to their predecessors, and with the risk of seeing the same scenario repeating itself.

This type of managerial discontinuity, in particular when experienced repeatedly over a decade or so, is at the root of the maturity problems many large firms are facing around cyber security.

Over time, as almost nothing gets achieved at each iteration, the need to drive a fundamental transformation around security practices becomes more and more crucial, but creating true change dynamics

1 www.thedigitaltransformationpeople.com/channels/people-and-change/the-ciso-merry-go-round/

also becomes more and more complex, as management gets frustrated and security becomes a problem and a failed topic.

The whole situation questions the average profile of the CISO as much as it does the appetite of their management for security.

In particular where driving a fundamental transformation programme around security practices is a key objective, the CISO needs to be an executive with the right amount of management experience, personal gravitas and political acumen. This cannot be a job for a technology hobbyist, an ex-auditor or a life-long consultant.

With the right level of seniority should come a sense that "Rome wasn't built in one day": A sound and honest appreciation of the culture of the firm, the pace at which it might change and, as a result, a sound appreciation of the time it could take to turn things around. Also a sense that only a shared transformative vision – shared with senior management and stakeholders – can drive and sustain change over the mid to long-term.

It cannot take 2 years for the CISO to realise that they are in the wrong job: In fact, the first six weeks are key: Over that period, the new CISO would have met with their management and their team. they would have met with key stakeholders and developed a sense of the challenges ahead, including the cultural and geographical diversity of their new organisation. They would have built a sense of what needs to be done, where they are in terms of budgetary cycle and the resources they have or could claim to deliver.

If the points of divergence with their management are too salient, it is at this point they should leave, and they should have the management experience and self-confidence to see it that way. Of course, it does make the first six weeks in the new job hard and challenging, but it is also about building trust and only trust between the CISO and key stakeholders will sustain change.

Spending the first six weeks or the first six months putting off burning fires or politically pushing a technical agenda the business stakeholders don't quite understand is a recipe for building frustration, not trust: Constant firefighting downgrades the role of the CISO. Pushing an arbitrary technical agenda and focusing only on the resources to deliver it also downgrades the role of the CISO and takes the debate onto the political minefield of priorities: Every senior manager in the firm has their own views on what needs to be done next, their own pet project and their own political weight. This is something the new CISO should avoid.

Instead, they should spend their first six months building a coalition around a transformative agenda that is right for the firm, together with an execution framework and a governance model to deliver it. The whole exercise should clarify priorities, timeframes and resources for all stakeholders.

And it should give the new CISO a view over their tenure which should be commensurate to the task at hand. In most cases, it will spread well over the average 2 years and could point towards a 5 years horizon, maybe a 6 to 9 years horizon. Taking on a CISO role becomes a very significant career step under that light. Even more significant if we take into account the seniority requirements we are placing on the role which will make it necessarily a mid to late-career step.

As a result, the CISO will have to be incentivised to stay the course and executive management must remain consistent with the agreed direction of travel. It will be hard for firms where short-termism prevails, but those who achieve it should start breaking the spiral of security failure in which they were entrapped.

#16 GDPR and the DPO: Threats or levers for the CISO?

5 April 2018

The GDPR is not just about Security, but it has been dominating the life of many CISOs since last year.

Notoriously, the regulation contains only a few actual references to data security. Article 32 mentions the need to have "appropriate" technical and organisational measures in place to ensure a level of security "appropriate to the risk" and quotes "inter alia" a few possible measures (pseudonymisation, encryption etc…), but that's almost the only specific reference to security in the whole text.

The "appropriateness" of the technical and organisational measures in relation to the risk has to be understood in the context of Article 32, i.e. "taking into account" the elements listed in the article:

- "The state of the art
- The costs of implementation
- The nature, scope, context and purposes of processing
- The risk of varying likelihood and severity for the rights and freedoms of natural persons"

Article 32 also cross-references Articles 40 and 42 and allows the use of approved codes of conduct and certification schemes to demonstrate compliance, but those won't be in place for a while given the way approval is described in the mentioned articles.

Beyond the lack of explicit definitions for the key terms ("appropriate", "state of the art") over which the guidance from the WP29 has shed little light so far, what does that mean in practice for the CISO?

Frankly, it should change very little to their practice: The GDPR simply seems to endorse a risk-based approach to delivering up to date security good practices to protect personal data. It is an approach that should be in place in many firms to protect any type of sensitive data (personal or not).

Having security measures appropriate to the "nature, scope, context and purpose of processing" should be a perfectly normal way of working (you don't secure an e-commerce website in the same way you secure a back-office in-house accounting system). And the reference to the "costs of implementation" is simply a reality check and hints at something which happens all the time in real-life: Every CISO will be used to having security measures rejected by their business on grounds on costs.

Information security good practices and risk-based approaches have been well established for the best part of the last 15 to 20 years, and most large firms would have had fully functioning security teams in place for the best part of that period and would have spent collectively billions on security products and consultants. So why would a CISO be worried?

CISO and DPO: Allies or enemies?

Could it be that in spite of the billions spent, little demonstrable alignment to security good practices was actually achieved in real terms over the past decade in many large firms? (there is ample anecdotal evidence of that surrounding the Wannacry ransomware outbreak in May 2017).

Outside already regulated industries (where the role of compliance and audit departments has been better established for a long time), could it be that the CISO is now worried that they will have a DPO "breathing down their neck"? and that the threat of massive fines is going to change the managerial dynamics of the game in favour of the DPO, who – in addition – benefits from a somehow protected regulatory status?

Of course, it depends on the profile of the individuals involved and we have analysed several times since 2015 the profile of CISO roles, their reporting lines and the type of interaction they can drive across large firms.

Where the CISO role is positioned as a "Change Agent" (in the language of those earlier articles), there should be little friction with the DPO and the GDPR offers fundamental levers to the transformational CISO.

The DPO is likely to be a new player in the security governance game, and it could be that he/she brings a different outlook and a different background to the table (very often it is likely to be somebody with some form of legal training).

The DPO will face many challenges similar to those faced by the transformational CISO around driving cultural change and engineering new dynamics around "privacy by design".

Working together, they can be strong allies if they manage to build and push from different angles a common transformative agenda and create together the structures they will need to demonstrate GDPR compliance (for the DPO) and ensure the adequate protection of information assets (for the CISO).

Where the CISO role is positioned as a "Firefighter" or a "Figurehead", the situation could be quite distinct: To both, the DPO could start demanding answers to difficult questions around the actual structure of their practice or its tangible output, and their relationship could become complex.

In all cases, the GDPR brings an opportunity to rethink Infosec and where necessary make it work better.

The role of the CISO is often the result of organic evolutions going back a decade or more. The new role of the DPO cannot exist on its own and will require a proper governance model to function and bring value to the whole organisation, despite its imposed independence.

They need to converge into a coherent operating model which builds on positive interactions between the functions, while respecting the constraints of each.

A considerable challenge, in particular in large firms, but a necessary one, and absolutely key to ensuring ongoing GDPR compliance post May 25th and adherence to the "privacy by design" objectives which are at the heart of the regulation.

#17 The Digital Transformation and the Role of the CISO[1]

9 July 2018 [with Vincent Viers]

Cybersecurity needs to be at the heart of the digital transformation, but organisational models will have to evolve

Cybersecurity is in the process of becoming an essential component of any organisation's digital transformation journey. There is no way around this, especially as policymakers start dipping their toes into privacy and security issues, and societal norms are shifting on the topic.

In fact, privacy and security considerations are the key ingredients of digital trust and must be at the heart of any industry's digital transformation. Far from being solely technological issues, they encompass for many firms profound cultural and governance issues.

The necessarily transversal nature of security and privacy matters needs to be woven into the fabric of an organisation for the digital transformation to succeed over the long-term, and this will force existing organisational models to evolve.

Of course, most new technology layers enabling the digital transformation need to be protected from interference, intrusion, or corruption. This is especially the case across industry sectors seeking to take advantage of the enormous opportunities offered by driverless vehicles and the logistics sector – amongst others – could be unrecognizable in ten years' time.

New technologies will also generate and feed on massive amounts of data – most of it sensitive or private – that will need to be collected, processed, and safeguarded in a way that is both sensible and ethical. This is absolutely key for example in the retail sector where the growing trends towards the enhanced personalisation and the

---

1 Originally published as an abbreviated version on the Kuppinger Cole blog; "The Digital Transformation and the Role of the CISO", July 2018 (https://www.kuppingercole.com/blog/guest/the-digital-transformation-and-the-role-of-the-ciso)

Fig. 5: Digital transformation and the logistics sector

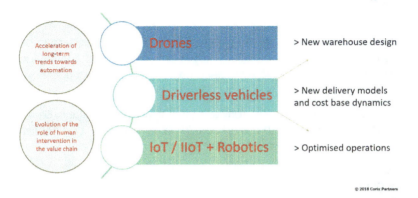

digitalisation of the consumer's journey are literally turning the industry on its head.

The concepts of security by design and of privacy by design will inevitably become any organisation's best allies in its innovative endeavours and must be taken seriously by all digital transformation players, especially as the regulatory and social contexts become harder to navigate.

Fig. 6: Digital transformation and the retail sector

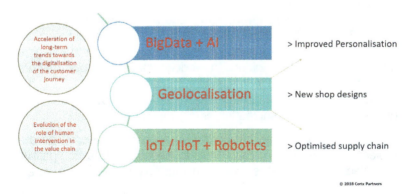

As data is increasingly becoming the fuel of the digital value-chain, it needs to be understood and treated as a truly valuable asset by all firms and protected as such.

But this must not be seen as a mere technical matter: It needs to be addressed across the corporate spectrum as a full managerial and cultural matter and could have deep organisational implications.

There is no doubt – in our opinion – that organisations which put information security and privacy at the heart of their digital transformation from the start could obtain a real competitive advantage in the mid-to-long run.

As a matter of fact, the recent launch of the General Data Protection Regulation (GDPR) in the EU is changing dramatically the incentives landscape for all businesses active in Europe.

Make no mistakes: The GDPR is an integral part of the digital transformation paradigm and illustrates how external forces – in this case, regulation – can and will be applied by politicians to try to restore market equilibrium – in this case, in the face of ruthless data monetisation – to protect the perceived interests of consumers and citizens.

Organisations can now be fined up to 4% of their global turnover for non-compliance but may be faced over the short-term with incoherent rulings and shifting legal norms (as nobody really knows yet how the regulators will act in practice). In addition, firms are now required to report any relevant data breach to the regulator within 72 hours. This will require capabilities of detection, analysis and reaction, which go far beyond the scope of the security teams and will force many corporate stakeholders to work together on those matters (security, IT, legal, DPO teams, senior management etc…). As such, the GDPR could be a painful lesson as to why cybersecurity is necessarily a transversal matter for organisations of all sizes.

Finally, and perhaps most importantly, respect for privacy and the protection of personal data is likely to become a true competitive advantage as our societies become increasingly warry of these issues.

This shift is well illustrated by the first complaints filed under the GDPR framework. Privacy activists such as Max Schrems or the French Quadrature du Net, for example, have already started to drag high-profile tech companies (Facebook, Google, Instagram, etc...) into what could become lengthy legal proceedings. Depending on how the regulators react, this could have deep implications on how data-driven businesses are to operate in Europe.

As consumers and other stakeholders start scrutinising more and more corporate attitude towards data, failing to acknowledge their concerns over these privacy issues – or worse, making the headlines when the next scandal hits – could do more harm to any business than a regulator's fine.

At the heart of those matters lies a deep reliance on digital trust. Once broken, it is the entire digital value chain which collapses...

Investors themselves are starting to regard digital trust is the true "secret sauce" of the digital transformation, and security and privacy – as its key ingredients – are fast becoming serious components at the heart of any sound ESG framework.

Increasingly, security and privacy become intertwined, but it makes little sense from a corporate governance perspective to allow a new privacy organisation under a DPO to grow in parallel to – or in conflict with – existing security structures. Synergies are obvious and need to be leveraged, and where security practices are deemed dysfunctional or in need of improvement, this could provide an ideal opportunity.

In fact, it could be the start of a major evolution around corporate perceptions of security and privacy, from burden, annoyance and costs, towards becoming central management functions.

But organisational models will have to evolve as a result to accommodate the truly transversal nature of security and privacy matters and carve out a niche for those new corporate functions.

At this junction, the traditional role of the CISO – heavily influenced by a technical bias, tactically-oriented and project-driven in many firms – could become exposed.

Not in its functional existence – IT security is more essential than ever – but in its corporate prominence. Having failed to project their roles beyond the tactical and technical fields for the best part of the last decade, many CISOs could find themselves pushed down the organisation while CSO and DPO roles take centre stage at the top.

Fig. 7: A new transversal organisational model

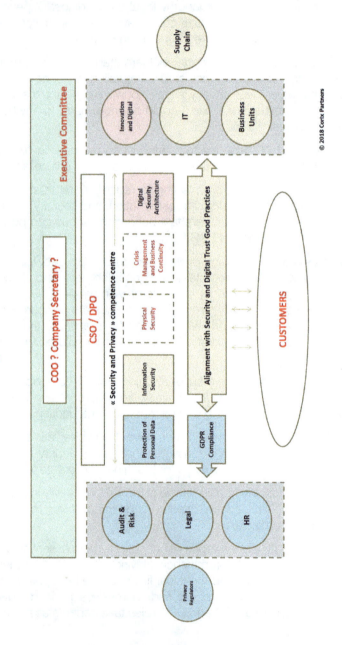

A New Transversal Organisational Model

© 2018 Corix Partners

With those new roles should come new people and a new focus, and probably a different way to approach security matters and talk about them.

We could be at the start of an exciting decade for all security professionals.

#18 Who wants to be a CISO?

3 January 2019

Talent alienation is the biggest issue behind the cybersecurity management skills gap, but it shouldn't be the case

Who wants to be a CISO these days? And at which stage in your career should you consider the move? What balance of managerial and technical experience do you need to have? And where do you go from there? (what's the step after next? … always the most important question in terms of career development)

Those would be valid questions for many executive positions but when it comes to the role of the CISO, they seem to acquire a different meaning.

Let's evacuate the first two aspects from the start: Cybersecurity has developed a high profile in many organisations over the past few years. Many firms are engaged in transformation programmes in that space, which will require strong leadership, transversal vision and managerial and political acumen from the CISO. The role is no longer a role for a junior technologist, an ex-auditor or life-long consultant. Of course, control-mindedness and a solid understanding of the technical aspects relevant to their industry sector are important, but they must not be seen as the only key aspects.

It's the "step after next" question which seems to be the dominant factor preventing people from moving into CISO jobs.

Security still carries an image problem, in spite of the high-profile of some recent cyber incidents and the undeniable interest developed by top executives around the topic over the past few years (and the additional layer of emphasis brought in by the GDPR).

It is still seen by many as a highly specialised field and a dead-end, plagued by under-investment and management lip service, where you cannot really achieve anything.

This is becoming wrong on all fronts, in particular in large firms involved in fundamental transformation programmes around cyber security:

Security can no longer be seen as a specialised technical silo. It is a transversal discipline rooted in corporate culture and governance which will take the CISO in contact with IT, business, HR, legal, risk and compliance functions. The digital transformation and the "security and privacy by design" principles coming with GDPR accentuate that trend even further. Only by looking at security in that way can large scale transformation programmes be truly successful.

The under-investment and lip-service era is behind us in many firms: Cyber security is on the Board agenda and "are we spending enough on cyber?" is becoming one of the most common question at that level. And the GDPR brings business-threatening fines of unprecedented proportions which can turn cynical lip-service into an expensive habit. Priorities and resources are shifting towards cyber security, but with those come management expectations and execution responsibilities for the CISO.

As a consequence of the two points above, large scale cyber security transformation programmes can be very complex and very exposed. They are nothing but a dead-end. They are exceptional training grounds and prime areas where ambitious leaders can develop and prove themselves to the Board.

Of course, ambition is required; and realism around the timeframes involved with delivering lasting change: It could take 3 to 5 years – or longer – to turnaround a security practice and that would make it a significant career step for the individual involved, but the role of the transformational CISO has all attributes to attract the best talents, and it is now down to the Board to raise its profile so that it does.

This goes beyond compensation and reporting lines: It is time for role models to emerge to illustrate that the successful transformational CISO is not condemned to hopping from one CISO job to another but can move into CIO, CRO or CDO roles, or indeed any leadership position where strong turnaround skills are required.

#19 The Impossible Role of the CISO
20 June 2019

Security Organizations must evolve. The CISO cannot be credible on all fronts

A recent comment I read on Linkedin made me think.

It was in response to a post on zero-day vulnerabilities and software patching, and roughly translated from the French, it read as follows:

"One day, you stand in front of the Ex Co having to explain how the millions spent on cyber over the years have improved their level of protection; then you go back to your desk to discover that 3 new vulnerabilities have just turned up which need patching across the entire estate; Welcome to my world !!!"

While I accept this reflects the life of many CISOs, it attracts comments at two levels:

First of all, if the "millions spent on cyber over the years" had been spent in the right places, none of the issues highlighted here should be a challenge for the CISO.

A cyber security practice needs to be a structured practice built around people and processes, supported by technology. Reporting capabilities should be embedded in it and inform any management decision up to the board. You build those over time. It requires mid to long-term vision and leadership from the CISO, but that's how the "millions" should have been invested over the years: People, Process THEN Technology.

Of course, many cyber security practices have been built the other way round: Jumping straight at the first technology solution every time something happens or at the first sight of an audit point, buying some tech product to address alleged quick wins, then wrapping processes around the capabilities of the product ... just to discover that you can't justify the resources to operate the way the product needs to be operated (before complaining endlessly about management and budgets; at which point the CISO generally moves on to their next job...)

This cannot carry on. Short-term focus on non-existent quick wins has led to a product proliferation problem which is simply killing security operations practices, and many large organizations are nowhere near the level of security maturity they should have reached with regards to the amounts invested over the last 10 to 15 years.

Many CISOs are simply trapped in endless projects, tactical games and firefighting. They struggle to see the bigger picture, while at the same time, many senior executives have now entered the "when-not-if" era and expect real action.

Meanwhile, breaches keep happening and over time, distrust sets in between business and security leaders. This spiral of failure also breeds a talent alienation dynamics and security problems can rapidly become self-perpetuating.

Organizations which find themselves in such situation must look back without complacency at the roadblocks which have prevented progress in the past around security matters: Invariably, they will be rooted in culture, governance and managerial short-termism.

To break this deadlock, they will have to attract and inject raw management talent into the security equation, and to that effect, current security organizations will have to evolve. Which takes me to my second point, in relation to the Linkedin comment I started from.

The CISO role which it refers to – although very real today in many organizations – is inherently flawed.

Nobody can be reasonably expected to be GENUINELY and EFFECTIVELY credible from the board down, across all managerial and technical layers of the enterprise, and transversally across all its silos, from HR to Legal, Procurement or Compliance – and of course across all geographies and cultures for global firms.

This profile simple does not exist (or is so rare it's not worth looking for). Yet, in many organizations, it is a little bit what is expected of the CISO, partly because of the inherently transversal nature of security, partly because no-one else appears to be relaying the security message.

This also cannot carry on: Security organizations in large firms have to restructure themselves in depth to encompass and structure all relevant disciplines and allow each of those to develop as it should, at its level.

Within a structured organization, roles should be defined and distributed to attract the best: The person talking to the board on security matters and the person making sure the IT estate is patched should not – and cannot – be the same.

In this context, the traditional role of the CISO will have to evolve, and probably leave the centre stage to a broader CSO role, which could be used to attract and develop a new generation of leaders into security roles.

This is absolutely necessary to address the transversal nature of security – and privacy – matters in large firms, and break the spiral of failure which has plagued cybersecurity for the last decade.

#20 The Tactical Trap

18 July 2019

Cyber Security maturity stagnates because many CISOs are structurally prevented from looking beyond day-to-day firefighting

Many CISOs struggle to look beyond day-to-day firefighting and get trapped in tactical games. We highlighted this last year in the context of our "100 Days" series and it is one of the major factors preventing organisations from developing better levels of cyber security maturity.

In many firms, this goes beyond incidents and the natural need to address those: It is often compounded by 3 structural elements literally trapping the CISO in tactical games, forcing endemic short tenures and creating the conditions for a systemic spiral of failure around cyber security.

First, corporate short-termism, which is still prevalent in many organisations amongst senior executive communities:

"In the long term, we're all dead" and anything that would not impact the next quarter figures does not grab interest for very long. Cyber security matters are being pushed towards those levels of management by non-stop media reports around data breaches and the potential level of GDPR fines, but when faced by multi-year, 7 or 8 digits transformative programmes of work around security that would genuinely force the firm to alter the way it works, those executives often revert to what they've been doing for decades around compliance: Looking for quick-wins and cheap boxes to tick so that they can "show progress" while minimising spend and disruption.

The problem with cyber security, is that organisations facing that type of problems are generally in need of a structural overhaul of their security practices, and "quick wins" are often non-existent. Driving real and lasting change takes time. Simply "fixing" illusory quick wins has never been the base of any transformation.

Second, plain old office politics between IT and Security which have always been a component of the life of many CISOs, irrespective of their reporting line (and this is undoubtedly worse where the CISO does not report to the CIO):

Technologists are trained and incentivised to deliver functionality, not controls, and many, over the past decades, have developed a culture which sees security measures as constraints instead of requirements.

Many CISOs are constantly bombarded by "urgent" requests to define security measures coming from IT people who should know better but are just "passing the buck".

The CISOs often feel that they would fail by not responding, not realising that this is a game they cannot win, and a form of political and emotional blackmail which must be avoided, especially outside large organisations where teams and resources tend to be smaller: The CISO and their team simply cannot be expected to be deep technical security experts on all technology streams and across all platforms, or to "drop everything" at any time to help projects.

Of course, they can rely on external skills (budgets permitting), but fundamentally roles, responsibilities and demarcation lines should be clear, and resources placed where they should be: The security of IT systems should be the responsibility of the respective IT teams. The security team should assist, validate and control while retaining a degree of independence. This is the spirit of all organisational models developed over the past 20 years around IT security. It should be clear and the CISO and their boss should have the backbone to enforce it.

Finally, in many cases, the greed of the tech industry, which is only aggravating the situation:

For each of those alleged "quick wins" or "urgent" issue to fix, there are countless vendors bidding to sell their stuff to put a tick in that box, irrespective of any bigger picture.

This is a pressure the CISO must resist. Over time, this accumulation of point solutions simply leads to a product proliferation problem which makes everything more difficult for the CISO and their team: From incident management to compliance reporting, security operations become burdened by the need to collect data across multiple platforms often in inconsistent formats, resources requirements escalate, and it aggravates the perception that security is just a cost and a pain, instead of a necessary barrier against real and active threats.

The CISO and IT must build the discipline to work with a small number of security vendors and service providers around which they can structure effective and efficient security operations, properly segregated, proportionate to the threats the business is facing and the resources available to fight them.

Clarity of roles and responsibilities across Security and IT, and a clear approach putting People and Process first ahead of ready-made Technology solutions, are the basis on which the CISO can avoid the tactical trap. It is also the only basis over which cyber security maturity can grow, across any organisation, large or small.

#21 Towards a New Profile for the CISO

12 September 2019

A decade of firefighting has taken its toll on the CISO profession

The role of the CISO is changing. If that was ever the case, it can no longer be seen JUST as a technical role.

In some industries, it is being challenged by the world-wide tightening of regulations around privacy and the emergence of DPOs and other related roles.

Everywhere, it is being challenged by the non-stop avalanche of cyber-attacks and data breaches of the past decade, which have raised the visibility of cyber security to Board level, but at the same time have also prevented many CISOs from getting out of fire-fighting mode.

This is the crux of the matter.

Senior executives are increasingly endorsing a "when-not-if" paradigm around cyber-attacks and are demanding fundamental change and action beyond day-to-day fire-fighting, often in exchange of very significant investments around security.

They are expecting the CISO to lead such programmes of work, but many CISOs have never been recruited or trained for such a challenge, under such level of scrutiny.

Very often, it is about addressing problems rooted in a decade of lip service or under investment around security, and it involves a true transformation of many business practices across the firm.

You don't become a transformational leader overnight, in particular if your background, your skills and your core interests are centred around the more technical aspects of cyber security. Nothing wrong with that, and while the focus was on fire-fighting cyber-attacks all the time, those would have been valuable qualities.

But as the focus shifts towards transformation and execution, the ability to influence across silos and to understand the true nature of the business and the more transversal aspects of security, becomes paramount. Those are rarely attributes of a native technologist, and they are not attributes you develop through the constant fire-fighting of technical problems.

So parallel to the "lost decade" of cyber security and reflecting it, there is also a lost decade for the CISO profession. A lost decade during which many have hopped from job to job, collecting higher and higher salaries for their technical firefighting skills, but without encountering the terrain in which to develop true enterprise-level leadership and transformational skills.

As senior executives turn a page and we enter – possibly – an execution-dominated decade around cyber security, many CISOs are just not equipped to lead.

Let's say this one more time: Just throwing money at cyber security problems won't make them disappear overnight. Remediating issues rooted in a decade of adverse prioritisation by the business will cost money, but it will also require time and in many cases, relentless drive to change mindsets.

Who should do this, if the CISO can't? … There are broadly 2 types of options:

Organisational models may need to evolve to allow a broader CSO type of role to emerge in large firms, encompassing security at large, continuity and privacy, with the CISO role retreating back to its technical roots. This would by itself attract a different calibre of individual into each role and such rebalancing of skills could be key to the success of large-scale cyber security transformation programmes.

Alternatively, the profile of the CISO needs to change to adjust to the imperatives of the "when-not-if" era: It becomes essential to start prioritising leadership skills over technical skills and distribute roles across a structured function, instead of looking for "unicorn" profiles: Nobody can be credible on all fronts all day long from the Board down, and horizontally across all functions and geographies of the business. Those profiles don't exist and pretending otherwise is just setting the CISO to fail.

#22 The Real Leadership Challenges around Cyber Security

9 January 2020

The World Economic Forum's "Cyber Security Guide for Leaders in Today's Digital World[1]" (WEF – October 2019) makes interesting reading, but frankly does it move the needle?

It does provide a solid and up to date summary on cyber security good practices and rightly puts a strong emphasis on the cultural aspects and the importance of trust.

It acknowledges the execution failure around cyber security ("current approaches make it difficult to implement comprehensive best practices across the full extent of the digital and operating environments in organizations") which is at the heart of what we have been calling the "lost decade", as well as the product proliferation problem which is plaguing the industry as a whole – and the lives of many CISOs and their teams ("although organizations have many tools in place (…), the tools often cannot be used in concert").

It also acknowledges the transversal nature of security matters, and the pressing need for the CISO and their teams to work across corporate silos, with support functions, business units, business partners and suppliers, and to build trust with each of those.

But in essence, it says very little around how to get things done, and that's the crux of the matter.

Many of those issues have been on the table for years. Some of the best practices pushed by the report – around inventories, patching, identity, continuity or crisis management for example – would have been included in similar reports 10 years ago.

So the real question is still very much: Why are so many large organizations still struggling with those? And how to remove the roadblocks which have prevented them from making progress over such a long period of time, in spite of colossal investments?

---

1   https://www.weforum.org/reports/the-cybersecurity-guide-for-leaders-in-today-s-digital-world

We wrote on this very matter for the first time in 2015, echoing an article from McKinsey ("Repelling the Cyber Attackers[1]" – July 2015) and an earlier WEF report, also co-authored with McKinsey ("Risk and Responsibility in a Hyperconnected World" – January 2014).

The 2019 report makes the right diagnostic around execution as we pointed out above but overlooks significantly the real challenges involved in getting things right, and their real underlying governance and human dimension.

The security industry needs to pivot away from "talking about things" and why they go wrong, onto "getting things done" and fixing things. This is not a problem which has – or can have – a purely technological solution.

Leadership and the profile of the leaders – NOT TECHNOLOGY – are at the heart of the execution paradigm around cyber security in today's digital world.

People trust other people, and you need the right leaders to get things done around security, with the right balance of technical understanding, management acumen, personal gravitas and emotional intelligence.

Where do you find such people, in a context where there are hardly any role models around and most CISOs are technologists by background?

To get them out of business roles seems the right approach, but to incentivize the right profiles, security roles have to be elevated to attract and retain the best. And to that effect, organizations and governance models have to evolve, as we pointed out in 2018.

A clear and solid governance model established upfront is key to driving any type of large scale security transformation programme, and old clichés such as "cyber security (being) everyone's responsibility in an organization" are totally meaningless in absence of clear roles and responsibilities, reflected in job descriptions and pegged to annual objectives and compensation schemes, at all levels up to the Board.

---

1 https://www.mckinsey.com/business-functions/mckinsey-digital/our-insights/repelling-the-cyberattackers

Those are the real challenges in today's digital world, as the focus shifts for senior executives, away from risk and compliance considerations towards the real execution and delivery of protective measures.

For too long, the security industry has been talking about what goes wrong without focusing enough on making sure that protective measures are in place. This is actually reflected directly – and quantitatively – in our 2019 semantics analysis of 17 annual "Global Information Security Surveys" from EY spanning a period from 2002 to 2019, with keyword markers such as "risk", "threat", "compliance" or "incident" 3.5 times more frequent across all surveys than words like "governance", "budget", "delivery", "priority", "culture" or "skill".

Threats evolve constantly, but old and well-established security basics do go a long way to ensure protection in many firms: In the face of escalating cyber-attacks and increasing regulatory pressure, the challenges around cyber security are no longer about knowing what to do, but to get it done, and to get it done now and for good.

#23 "Good Security Governance" is not a Piece of Useless Consultant Jargon

12 March 2020

It is an essential protective layer for any organisation.

Irrespective of what many of us may say or write, the cyber security agenda remains dominated by products and technology.

Of course, the problem has a technical dimension and the protection of any firm against cyber threats will require the application of technical countermeasures at a number of levels.

But there are countless tech vendors and service providers out there trying to sell their products as the silver bullet which will protect you from anything. And countless small firms still holding simplistic views on cyber threats: "We're fine; all our data is in the cloud"

For any organisation above a certain size, effective and efficient protection can only result from the layered application of protective measures at people, process and technology level. And in that order.

It has to start with people. And that doesn't mean rolling out a security awareness programme. Middle management has always had the tendency to jump straight into the solution space at the back of a simplistic analysis of the problem, but at the heart of the "people" aspects of any security strategy, lay issues of corporate culture and corporate governance.

"Good security governance" is not a piece of useless consultant jargon. It is an essential protective layer for any organisation.

It ensures a visible endorsement of security values from the top down, brings clarity around security roles, responsibilities and accountabilities across the whole organisation, and more importantly, it is the cornerstone that "get things done" around security through an effective and efficient layer of reporting.

Only the actual execution of security measures (i.e. the actual deployment of security processes and the technology required to support them) will protect the business. And that's where many organisations – larger and smaller – have failed over the past decades in spite of colossal investments in cyber security: Security projects get deprioritised half way through or focus only on non-existent low hanging fruits; over time, people get demotivated and leave, nothing gets finished and half-baked "solutions" proliferate: According to a recent survey by Cisco, the average organisation now uses 20 different security technologies.

Let's get this straight: This is plain governance failure and it has been plaguing organisations – large and small – around security for the best part of the last two decades.

To avoid those mistakes, break that spiral, and target the management and governance roadblocks which have prevented progress in the past, most organisations need to act at three levels:

First, get a good understanding of your security maturity posture to start with and set realistic timeframes around change. Change takes "the time it takes" and there may be no quick wins.

Then, be objective about the skills and resources you have to deliver change and set realistic improvement goals. Jumping straight at ineffective "virtual CISO" solutions in the hope of making the problem disappear will not help if nobody is there to execute.

Finally, stay focused. Security transformation often involves a change in mindset which needs stability to develop and takes time to set in. Changing directions or priorities every time something happens in the business or elsewhere will simply kill any transformational momentum around security.

#24 The CISO must be – first and foremost – a Leader

29 October 2020

The key challenges of the transformational CISO are not technological, but managerial.

There is still a vast amount of debate across the cyber security industry about the role of the CISO, their reporting line, their tenure, the levels of stress they're under, and the burnout epidemy they're suffering.

But looking into the actual profile of real people in those jobs, talking to them and listening to their problems, you'd quickly realise that there is a fair amount of creative writing involved in a lot that's being posted.

It is easy to write about "the CISO" thinking this is a fully established C-level role and one of the pillars of corporate governance. In practice, this is far from being the case and the harsh reality is that the role itself is far from mature, in spite of having been in existence – in some shape or another – for about two decades.

The job title – to start with – is far from universal (and has never been). A large number of variants are in use, and behind those, different role descriptions reflecting the perceptions and priorities of each organisation, which in turn find themselves reflected in the reporting line of the function.

Compounded by the natural differences between industry sectors and the security maturity levels of each company, it creates a myriad of roles, which – in the end – can have very little in common.

The actual reality of the role of a "CISO" reporting to a board member in a mining firm, will have very little to do with the role of a "CISO" reporting 2 levels below the CIO in a retail organisation. Even if good practices are the same – and have been for a long time, and still protect – putting them in place in each of those situations will have very different meanings.

So talking about "the CISO" is often a dangerous shortcut when trying to address the functional or operational aspects of the role.

Where there are commonalities, is around the softer aspects of the role.

First of all, if an organisation is large enough to frame the role in CISO terms, it is likely the CISO will have a team below them. This is where many articles on the theme often go wrong: They talk about "the CISO" as if he or she was a one-man (woman) band, directly involved in the delivery of all aspects of their cyber security practice. That's rarely the case. In most organisations, the CISO is effectively a leader, structuring, organising, delegating and orchestrating work across their team and across the firm – and across the multiple third-parties involved in delivering or supporting the business.

The CISO should also be expected to be able to listen to business leaders across corporate silos, understand their priorities, and adjust security practices to their demands and expectations.

It is simply absurd to pretend that the CISO should have those managerial skills, and – at the same time – expect them to constantly put out burning fires, and be credible all the time and all the way across all technical stacks and across all silos of a large corporate. These unicorn profiles simply don't exist.

What is not absurd is to expect the CISO to structure and lead a team which can be credible on all those fronts – and firefight, and bring along long-term change. That's the only way it can work in large firms.

Senior executives also need to understand the complexities involved in leading true security transformation across large corporates, and accept the gaps which may exist at times between knowing what needs to be done to protect the business, saying it should be done and making sure it gets done, for good and across the real breadth and depth of the enterprise.

In bridging those gaps, lie the real challenges of the role of the transformational CISO. Those are not technological challenges, but managerial, political and governance challenges.

To be successful, the transformational CISO needs to be – first and foremost – a leader with a good business brain. Not just a firefighting technologist.

The CISO
and the CIO

#25 The 3 Cyber Security Governance Challenges of the CIO[1]

3 February 2015 – 21 April 2016

How does information security end up in the portfolio of the CIO?

Historically, the CIO has ended up in charge of information security in many organisations because many tactical measures required to deal with cyber threats lie in the IT field.

For decades, executive management has lived with the perception that information security breaches have a low frequency and a low impact. To be fair, the size of the risk map which board members have to respond to has increased enormously over the past 10 to 15 years – and today, information-related risks are still just one small part of that overall risk map. Geopolitical and financial risks have escalated, as well as environmental risks – which have become more and more prominent in recent years. When coupled with endemic short-termist or compliance-obsessed management tendencies, cyber risks have often failed to be picked up on the board of directors' radar up to now.

Occasionally, the topic might have been escalated by auditors or regulators, but overall it was seen as part of the normal way of running a large and complex organisation where many things can go wrong every day.

A number of very high profile data breaches in recent years (Target, Sony, Ashley Madison, Talk Talk etc…) have started to change that perception. However, many board members still tend to see cyber security breaches as something technical they don't really understand.

---

1 Originally published on the C-Suite blog; « Information Security: Three Governance Challenges for the CIO This Year », February 2015 (http://www.thecsuite.co.uk/CIO/index.php/security/210-governance-challenges-for-cio-4435435)

Can the CIO make a difference?

With the right attitude, the CIO can be a real driving force behind significant information security improvements.

In our opinion, it is not necessary to be overly concerned with "separation of duties" considerations. In most organisations, the CIO is a respected executive – as either a board member or reporting directly to a board member – and is entrusted with the management of large teams and very significant budgetary responsibilities.

The risk is often greater for an arbitrary separation of duties to fuel internal politics and paralyse effective decision making.

What are the factors shaping the relationship between information security and the CIO?

First of all, the CIO needs to be control-minded for the relationship to function, or at least should have an interest in information security matters and some grasp of the concepts involved.

If the CIO is not personally or politically capable of looking beyond financial or IT delivery matters, information security will often be delegated down and, over time, turn into a mere box-checking exercise.

While this may randomly protect the organisation to a level which satisfies executive management, it will also perpetuate the poor practice belief that cyber threats aren't really that important – with auditors and regulators continuing to run the control agenda.

This is a situation which we observe constantly in the field, with organisations failing to properly address the ongoing threats they face – in spite of spending huge sums of money on audit or compliance-driven programmes of work, or in knee-jerk response to incidents.

If the CIO is control-minded and wants to make a difference, he or she needs a clear definition of their information security role and a clear remit.

It's important to remember that information does not only exist in digital form. It also has a physical form, and more importantly it is constantly manipulated by people as part of business processes. When it comes to personal information, there is often a complex legal framework to comply with, particularly for global organisations.

Protecting information requires concerted action at a physical, functional and technical level. But the CIO can only be directly responsible for the technical aspects of information protection.

How does a CIO implement a successful approach to information security?

The CIO needs to send the right messages in three directions: upwards, downwards and sideways – and will face key management challenges in each case.

Managing upwards: How to engage with board members on information security matters?

CIOs will find that executive management is becoming more and more receptive to the cyber security messages being hammered out by politicians and the media. Board members might also have been scared by recent data breaches and the aggressive media coverage that surrounded them.

Many board members have started to understand that, even if significant information security breaches still have a relatively low frequency (all things considered), this frequency has increased dramatically over recent years. In addition to this, the impact information security breaches can have has become more and more difficult to quantify due to the increasing dependency on third-parties and the tremendous amount of media and political interest that has been building up. Losses can easily run into the tens of millions and – more importantly – brand reputation and customer trust can be left irrecoverably damaged by cyber- attacks.

The message from the CIO to the board must be clear: Where the problem is rooted in decades of neglect, under investment and adverse prioritisation, there can be no miracle solution, technical or otherwise: Avoiding these breaches, or dealing with them, will require coherent action over time – across the whole organisation. For this to be successful, each party involved (business units, HR, Legal, IT, etc...) needs to have a clear understanding of its role and remit.

This is why a medium to long-term strategy and a solid cross-silo governance model are essential to drive cyber security transformation. Ideally, it should also include a commitment from the board to medium to long-term funding, in order to allow all parties to plan information security delivery over the necessary timeframes.

The first challenge of the CIO is to drive this message upwards in the organisation – to the board of directors and its members.

Cyber security is also inherently a global problem, and only with a clear and unambiguous vision – coming from the top – can the CIO be successful at delivering complex technical security platforms across all operational divisions and geographies of a large organisation.

Managing downwards: How do you close the gap between security and IT?

At the same time, CIOs must look without complacency at their own organisation.

Technologists are almost always trained and incentivised to prioritise delivering functionality, often seeing security controls as a pain point or a limitation to their work.

There is no natural cultural fit between security and IT. As a result, information security is rarely seen as a powerful career path – and it can even have the tendency to alienate talent.

The profile of the individual who is going to drive information security across the CIO's organisation and across the enterprise as a whole – the Chief Information Security Officer, or CISO – is fundamental.

Due of the inherent complexity and cross-silo nature of the topic, the CISO must be an experienced executive with a significant management background and gravitas, as he or she will have to build internal respect and leadership in order to be successful.

The CISO will also face the task of addressing the short-term tactical problems that will unavoidably stem from incidents or legacy situations – while driving the medium to long-term information security vision the CIO should be building with executive management.

These are attributes of seniority that are fairly rare, internally or externally. The CIO is not likely to find them amongst young executives, ex-consultants or ex-auditors.

Acknowledging the specifics of the role and finding the right CISO is the second key challenge for the CIO – and the most difficult.

It will take time and may require the personal and political courage to look at current organisational arrangements and restructure them.

The reporting line of the CISO is also essential, with the lack of cultural fit between security and IT being a key element in that respect. In order to be taken seriously across an organisation, information security must be seen as a native part of the CIO's responsibilities – and it is absolutely essential for the CISO to have a direct reporting line to the CIO. Blending information security with the portfolio of another IT executive, or pushing the CISO role further down in the org charts, is simply a recipe for failure – fuelling the de-prioritisation of information security matters and further widening the gap between security and IT.

But, with the right seniority and profile, and at the right place in the CIO's organisation, the CISO – who should naturally navigate across corporate silos – can be a very powerful political ally for the CIO.

Managing sideways: How does the CIO lead themselves to success?

Finally, in order to be successful in establishing an effecting Information Security practice, the CIO must remain focused and in control of their own cyber security priorities over the medium to long-term.

Where cyber security problems are rooted in decades of adverse prioritisation or under investment, there can be no quick fix. Change can only take time and relentless drive.

Historically, audit functions have strongly interfered with the control agenda of many organisations and driven numerous tactical decisions – often justified by the absence of any strategic security vision or interest coming from executive management.

Now, it might be other senior stakeholders stepping in, asking for knee-jerk action in response to some high-profile data breach happening elsewhere.

The problem is that these people can also lack real life field experience, often causing them to single out arbitrary issues, ignoring the cyber security bigger picture and how complex it can be to get things moving in that space.

These arbitrary issues can confuse priorities, and can easily cause a long-term information security plan to head off on a tangent.

The third challenge faced by CIOs is in tackling this issue. The CIO needs to manage the relationship with auditors and senior stakeholders firmly and intelligently in order to remain in control of the cyber security agenda.

First, the CIO must ensure that all parties are aware of the broader control agenda set for the whole organisation, and of the vital need to work within it.

But the CIO must also have the confidence, together with the personal gravitas and political acumen, to push back on arbitrary issues that do not fit within the broader control agenda.

All this can only work as part of a coherent medium to long-term information security strategy and governance model –unambiguously signed off by all parties.

#26 Cyber Security and The Incoming CIO: What's Really Going On?

22 September 2016

Here is a scenario we are seeing far too often in the field: A new CIO comes in, identifies security problems, then nothing serious happens. At best, some tactical initiative would be pushed forward to answer outstanding audit issues, or a big gun of the industry called in to deliver countless slides out of which some hypothetical "quick wins" would be enacted to calm the Board about cyber risks.

Why so many incoming CIOs seem to be so cautious on cyber security at early stages of their tenure, in the face of glaring internal issues and constant reminders of data breaches in the news, is a worrying question. Their answers are invariably the same: They have "more pressing problems elsewhere", "bigger fishes to fry", "the business won't wear it", "budgets are too tight"; a new organisation is due to be announced "next week" or "next month", they'll "come to it" in due course, "next year", "once the new CEO has decided where priorities should be", etc…

In most large firms, those have to be seen as poor excuses: The CIO would often have hundreds of staff in their teams, tens of millions in annual budget, and a significant direct sign-off limit consistent with their Board-level reporting line. In a context where everything runs in parallel and everything costs money, the truth is that addressing cybersecurity shortcomings from the start is often a mere matter of priorities for any new CIO.

Priorities and personal courage, because the reality is that underlying security problems are invariably complex and involve a combination of organisational, technical and managerial issues:

Legacy InfoSec teams buried in the org chart, poorly staffed, poorly skilled forced into a constant, tactical and technical firefighting.

Expensive technical security initiatives half-deployed, poorly sold to business and IT staff because always designed as point solutions to specific problems in absence of any bigger picture, and as a result perceived as a burden and a waste of money.

Senior management very willing to accept cyber risk as a top risk for the firm, but at the same time, refusing to adhere for themselves to basic rules of security hygiene when it comes to mobile devices or passwords (rules that they are otherwise happy to impose on all other members of staff).

Standing up to the Board on those matters to tell them what they need to have, not just give them what they want, takes some gravitas, but should elevate the role of the CIO, not diminish it. For most large and complex firms, if cyber security maturity is low because nothing structured has ever been done in that space in the past, a data breach is merely a question of time. And, given current levels of media and political interest on these topics, gambling on it could be costly in a number of ways (financially or reputationally for the firm; personally for the CEO), as amply demonstrated by the TalkTalk data breach in the UK in 2015.

Not only is waiting for something to happen a dangerous game, but it often leads to absurd knee-jerk reactions which simply perpetuate the pre-existing short-termist approach to security without creating any fundamental change momentum.

Incoming CIOs should not be scared to launch into a cyber security transformation programme at early stages of their tenure if they see a need, and good governance around cyber security is fast becoming "the most important criterion for an organisation to feel well protected", as highlighted by a short survey from recruitment firm Boyden[1] collating feedback from 36 top CIOs.

Of course, there may be legacy people problems to resolve and those may take time, but overall, building a sound security organisation and operating model, able to reach and operate across the whole firm, is often the best start. Many security problems cut across corporate silos (into HR, legal, business disciplines) and a strong CISO with true management experience – not a mere firefighter, or a technology hobbyist – can be a strong ally for the CIO in broader transformational battles across IT or the business.

---

1 Boyden, "Cybersecurity: Is your Board on board?", 2016

#27 Why reporting to the CIO is increasingly a problem in large firms

16 June 2016

Our view – built on years of direct field experience – is that the reporting line of the CISO has to be at board level and must be driven by clear underlying objectives shared unambiguously by the CISO and their boss – whoever that happens to be in the organisation.

It could be a need to increase cyber security maturity. It could be a need to demonstrate compliance to regulators. It could be a need to demonstrate to shareholders that the right things are being done following a data breach. It could be all of the above… But in all cases, the boss has to be prepared and willing to throw their weight into the battle unambiguously and consistently.

In an ideal world, it's their boss' flawless commitment to cyber security values that the CISO does leverage on to drive change, coupled with their own gravitas, political astuteness and management acumen.

In our opinion, this articulation is the strongest to deliver lasting change, and is considerably stronger than multiple reporting lines or dotted lines, often aimed at avoiding perceived "conflicts of interest" but in practice poorly understood and highly vulnerable to internal politics.

However, it is also a construction which is coming under pressure in many firms when it comes to the relationship between the CIO and the CISO. And it is as a direct result of the pressure being applied to CIOs by executive management to deliver "digital transformation".

Many CIOs struggle – frankly – with such pressure. One day, they are told – by auditors or regulators – to focus on getting the basics right and keep legacy systems going. The next, they are told – by their board – to be more "agile", to work faster and to "do digital". And they have to square that circle with the teams they have – not necessarily best equipped in terms of skills – and often at the back end of several years of cost-cutting that might have introduced dysfunctional offshoring arrangements and opened the door to countless "shadow IT" situations within the business.

Where does cyber security fit in all this? Very often, the answer is quite obvious: It doesn't... until something goes wrong.

And it is exactly in this context that maintaining a reporting line to the CIO is increasingly a problem for the CISO. If the CIO is no longer able to prioritise cyber security all the time towards the top of the list because of the pressure of the "digital transformation", then the reporting line of the CISO must shift to another board member who can. And quickly.

This is a very serious matter because – precisely – the "digital transformation" itself is introducing at a very fast pace countless new cyber security issues – from customer data privacy considerations to the security of IoT devices. Those are best addressed from the start instead of retrofitted later. A strong CISO is key at times like these and can be an essential part to engineering cyber security as a competitive advantage. But they need to be highly visible in the organisation and backed unambiguously by a board member who cares.

#28 Reporting Line of the CISO: What Really Matters

4 May 2017

Corporate culture and the profile of the CISO are key, over and above any arbitrary organisational consideration

It is astonishing to see the amount of interest still surrounding the reporting line of the CISO. The fact that it is still a topic of serious discussions amongst security professionals is teaching us a few things about the role and its perception: Is the role properly established, identified and accepted in organisations? or is it (still) seen as some form of arbitrary (and bureaucratic) imposition by regulators?

In theory, there should be no debate in the face of a constant avalanche of cyber security issues in the news. The need to protect the firm from cyber threats should be obvious for the Board. One Board member should own the problem and delegate the coordination and delivery of the necessary protective measures to one of their direct reports. Period.

At this point, there are several options available for the reporting line, depending on the cyber security challenges the firm is facing and its digital footprint. Those lead to different role profiles for the CISO which we have analysed in an earlier article.

The right reporting line is always the one that works and get things done, not an arbitrary one that creates barriers, engenders politics and hinders delivery (even if it ticks audit or compliance boxes).

In practice, however, things rarely work so simply. It is not uncommon to encounter problems of understanding at Board level around cyber security issues, leading to adverse prioritisation. Equally, there are often skills issues at Board level minus 1, leading the difficulties in appointing a CISO with the right profile for the role. Looking externally often fails (in particular in large firms) because of the intrinsically horizontal nature of the CISO role, and the need to understand how the firm really works in order to navigate across corporate silos, be credible and make things happen around security.

All this often leads to placing the CISO role by default in the portfolio of the CIO or the CTO, even if those are not Board members.

This is not a problem in itself, in particular in firms that have a strong technological bias, and there are many good ways to make this work efficiently, as we have suggested in the past.

Many security professionals who have an interest in this topic seem concerned with separation of duties issues, and the fact that conflicts of priorities may emerge between the CISO and their boss in those configurations.

It is true that CIOs and CTOs are coming under a lot of pressure in relation with the digital transformation and some may struggle to dedicate time, attention or priorities to security matters. But it does not make the option a bad one by itself.

Culture is key in all this, as well the personality and the gravitas of the individuals involved.

In today's world, if a CIO or a CTO is not capable of prioritising in favour of cyber security matters in the face of constant incidents across all industry sectors, frankly it is likely that no-one in the firm will, and wherever you place the reporting line of the CISO, you will be encountering similar cultural issues. Those could be rooted in endemic short-termism, or very simply, in poor management or governance practices at the top.

But if the CIO or the CTO is cyber security aware and control-minded, then the CISO could become a very strong ally for them and help them forge a truly transformative vision.

Of course, the seniority and the gravitas of the individuals involved is essential. The CISO role is transversal and complex and needs to be given the right profile internally to attract the right senior professional. This is a role where real-life managerial experience is key to work autonomously, navigate around all pitfalls and fight the right political battles at the right time. All those aspects are probably more important than the raw technical skills.

This is not a job for a junior consultant, a junior IT executive or an ex auditor, irrespective of their potential. This is a hard job that requires an experienced pair of hands, with personal and political gravitas.

Issues around conflicts of priorities often emerge where both the CIO and the CISO lack that gravitas or political acumen: The CIO not willing to face the business over security issues, and the CISO not willing to confront the CIO over it. Those are not intrinsic issues that are inherent to the reporting line, but personal matters that relate to the managerial attitudes of those involved.

The CISO needs to be a credible field executive who really knows how the firm works, reporting to a control minded senior executive at Board level. Little else matters, and certainly not arbitrary separation of duties considerations.

#29 Why are we still talking about the reporting line of the CISO?

10 May 2018

The right reporting line is the one that works. Period.

Why are so many organisations and security professionals still worried about the reporting line of the CISO? This is one of the oldest and most consistent debate agitating the security industry, and it looks far from resolved.

It has been polluted for decades by arbitrary and simplistic views on "separation of duties" and alleged "conflicts of interest". But those views often come from sectors of the corporate spectrum with a fairly theoretical idea on how an organisation should operate, and rarely reflect the reality of how large organisations function.

The truth is that people work with people and that strong organisations are bound by trust, not distrust.

So the reporting line of the CISO must be a means, not an end. A means to enable the security practice of an organisation to deliver on its objectives, whatever those might be.

And that of course implies first that the security practice needs to have clear objectives: A clear sense of purpose, a mission statement, an operating and governance model, a mid to long-term roadmap with clear milestones. It cannot be just a random list of projects driven by audit observations.

The reporting line of the CISO must be high enough in the organisation for the CISO to be visible, audible and credible across all corporate silos, across all business units, across all geographies and with key vendors.

The solidity of the relationship between the CISO and their boss is paramount. It is the true cornerstone of the construction and the real key to success. It must be unquestioned and unquestionable. They must speak with one voice, share the same vision of what security means and needs to achieve, and the same appreciation of the timeframes involved.

And finally, the reporting line of the CISO must allow the right degree of independence and freedom for the CISO to remain able to act in all situations and arbitrate freely on conflicts and priorities. But that last point is only a parameter in this equation and must not rule alone.

Frankly, if security is not top of the list with the CIO, in a context where cyber incidents are at the top of the news several times a year, and often several times a month, it is likely that the CIO is simply the "tip of the iceberg", reflecting what the business units are pushing upon him, and if that is the case, wherever you place the reporting line of the CISO in the organisation, you might find similar problems.

The key is to elevate the debate away from simplistic views on "conflicts of interest" and root it in the reality of the firm and the objectives of the security function.

The reporting line of the CISO needs to be meaningful – not arbitrary –, positively determined and operated on a basis of trust between the CISO and their boss, unambiguous, stable over the mid to long-term and positioned at a level in the organisation where action can be taken, and resources prioritised. That means at Board level or Board minus one. NEVER below.

Those are the key factors: They will lead to different answers from one organisation to another, and that's perfectly normal. The right reporting line for the CISO is simply the one that works at enabling the security practice to do its job in the best possible way.

#30 Cyber Security and the Culture of Alienation

13 August 2020

Empirical, bottom-up and organically developed cyber security functions need to evolve

The 2020 Information Security Maturity Report[1] from ClubCISO makes interesting reading.

It compiles responses from 100 of their members to a questionnaire sent in March 2020, around the time of the COVID-19 lockdown decision in the UK. Comparing results year or year is not entirely meaningful for such surveys, in absence of any form of data normalisation (you have no guarantee that the panel responding is the same year on year); yet some interesting patterns emerge.

The typical respondent is a CISO working for a mid-size or large organisation (82% have more than 500 staff), headquartered in the UK or Ireland (75%), and has spent more than 10 years in the Infosec industry (69%); 60% have been in their present role for less than 2 years.

Collectively, they paint a slightly uncomfortable picture: The picture of CISO roles and security practices still operating bottom up, disconnected from the dynamics of the business: When asked which concerns most affect their ability to deliver against objectives, 49% mention the culture of the organisation (as if they were not part of it), 36%, the speed of business change (as if it was happening all around them but without them), 33%, the level of board support (although in response to another question, 58% say they would like to report to board level…).

It would be fascinating to ask some of the questions to the direct bosses of the respondents and compare results.

Of course, in such context of alienation from the business, budgets are hard to get by for CISOs (41% mention budgets as a main concern and 57% mention insufficient staff), frustration builds up and leads to

---

1 See https://www.clubciso.org/downloads/

attrition: When asked why they left their last role, 47% of respondents mention "not seeing eye to eye with senior leadership" (!), not having sufficient resources to make their role a success (in their view of course), or frustration with their organisation's approach to security.

But another shocking fact is that 89% of respondents say they don't have a security operating model in place (82% say they are working on one at varying degrees). This element alone puts the rest of the survey into perspective: In absence of a structured framework to work against, most cyber security practices can only operate "as they go along", in project mode or in firefighting mode: How can you justify budgets, attract or retain talent without a referential to work against , and in absence of a clear governance model, roles, responsibilities and – to a degree – clear career paths?

And again, how can you claim you do not have enough staff in absence of a target operating model, detailing tasks and the resources required to deliver those tasks? It can only be a finger-in-the-air exercise; the very kind any half-decent CFO would smell miles away.

This kind of empirical, bottom-up and organically developed cyber security function does not work and needs to evolve.

What is required is structure, business acumen and top-down engagement.

The emphasis on security culture throughout the report is valuable and meaningful, but it cannot be the only axis of action for the CISO: Security awareness has always been a low hanging fruit, and an easy sell for CISOs, when they cannot find other levers. You can't go very wrong by distributing mouse mats and leaflets, and it does not cost the world. But this is not what culture change is about. And there cannot be any culture change that does not come top-down.

The culture of alienation many CISOs have developed is probably comfortable for some; there is always someone to blame ("the business") and another juicy job to move into afterwards.

But it does not help organisations, and society at large.

To break this spiral of failure, the profile of the CISO needs to evolve and the board needs to take ownership.

This is no longer just about tech – if it ever was. This is about protecting the business against cyber-attacks which have now become a matter of "when, not if". This is no longer something you can push down in the organisation.

If the board does not see the need – or does not feel qualified – to step in, nothing will never change for good around cyber security because it has simply become too complex and too transversal. Bottom-up approaches will continue to pour cash down the drain and CISOs will continue to leave every other year out of frustration. And breaches will continue to happen.

If the board wants to set directions, they should drive: Appoint someone they trust and can talk to (it does not have to be a technologist), and empower that person to build or rebuild cyber security practices across the firm, in the light of what the board wants and expects.

The COVID crisis is presenting most organisations with unprecedented situations, but it does not make cyber security less of a priority. On the contrary, cyber security – whether it is in support of remote working, e-commerce or digitalised supply chains – will be a pillar of the "new normal".

Now is the time to deal with it strategically, and from the top down.

#31 A Different Take on The Short Tenure of the CISO

18 March 2021

Looking beyond stress, burnout, and scapegoating theories: What is really going on?

This good piece from Dan Lohrmann on GovTech around the tenure of the CISO made me think (Why Do Chief Security Officers Leave Jobs So Often? — 28 Feb 2021[1]).

Overall, Dan's analysis is comprehensive and the negative undertones behind the short tenure of CISOs match those in the ClubCISO 2020 Information Security Maturity Report on which we commented last year.

Still, I would frame the topic slightly differently, and I think an element of reflexion is also required on the impact the short tenure of CISOs is having on the security industry at large and the evolution of the cyber security maturity of large firms.

First of all, many firms, which never had a CISO before, have opened up new positions across the last decade, and demand is strong from industry sectors which were never real players in the security space.

When I started attending security conferences over 20 years ago, most of my peers were in Finance, big Pharma, or the Energy sector; regulated industries or industries where security has always worked hand in hand with safety, and where safety has always been a pillar of the culture of the sector.

Today, most industry sectors have some form of security practice in place. Recruitment activity around CISO roles is significant and profitable for recruiters. There is a significant shortage of quality management profiles in that space; salaries are high and are on the rise.

To put it simply, good CISOs get head-hunted — at least around me. Some offers are just "too good to turn down" and a number of them simply "follow the money".

---

1 https://www.govtech.com/blogs/lohrmann-on-cybersecurity/why-do-chief-security-officers-leave-jobs-so-often.html

But for others, things are rarely as straightforward, and here I would go back to Dan's analysis: The decision to change jobs is often rooted in a negative context, and the call from the recruiter is just the catalyst which starts the process. Again, this is clear in the ClubCISO 2020 Information Security Maturity Report: Out of the seven responses presented by the report to the question "Why did you leave your last role?" (p. 19), five are clearly and unambiguously negative: From the shocking "not seeing eye to eye with senior leadership", to "spending too much time firefighting", "not being compensated sufficiently", "being frustrated by the organisation's approach to security", or "not having enough resources or support to succeed".

Clearly, CISOs don't seem to be a very happy bunch, and their frustration appears to be rooted in some form of disconnect with their management.

That's understandable: Many CISO positions were created in response to rampant cyber threats across the last decade in industries which never had such roles in place. They were created tactically with the operational objective of preventing breaches, by senior executives who didn't really understand the context and the transversal complexity involved in the cyber protection of large organisations.

It created situations where many CISOs struggled with limited resources and constant attacks, and never managed to build a meaningful narrative with management beyond mere firefighting.

They might have hopped from job to job, but they carried the problem with them, and over the past decade, many CISOs have not been able to develop the leadership and management skills which they would need to elevate the role to the next level.

And in parallel, expectations from management have changed. In the face of constant breaches in the news, the penny has finally dropped in many boardrooms and the "when-not-if" paradigm around cyber-attacks has taken root. Many boards have reached the point where they are ready to make very significant transformative investments around cyber security, but in exchange, would demand faultless execution and delivery from their CISO.

That's what is putting many CISOs under unbearable pressure, because over the past decade, they have been prevented — by constant firefighting — from developing the softer skills, the personal gravitas, the political acumen, which are key to delivering complex initiatives in large firms.

To me, this is the context in which the short tenure of CISOs has to be seen. A survey by Nominet estimated it at 26 months in 2020. Anecdotal evidence from my network seems to back this up: Having analysed the Linkedin profile of 15 of my contacts currently in CISO positions, I have reached the figure of 30 months, each having held 3 different CISO position on average throughout their career.

It is time to start recognising the impact this CISO "merry-go-round" has had on the security industry over the past decade and on the evolution of security maturity in large firms.

You achieve very little in large organisations in 2 to 3 years, certainly very little that could have a lasting transformative impact — if that's what's required.

At best you kick start some projects, but each CISO comes in with their own culture, priorities and approach, and your successor may or may not follow in your footsteps. Over time, distrust sets in with senior management, who can't help but noticing that breaches keep happening in spite of the investments made in that space. Security becomes a cost and a problem; an area no ambitious executive, internally, would consider as a possible career step.

This distrust and the spiral of failure fuelled by CISOs short tenures are at the heart of the problem here, and over the last decade, the situation has become self-perpetuating.

As we wrote back in 2018, "nothing will change until the profile of the CISO is raised and they start to see their role over the mid to long-term".

To break this spiral, the Board needs to own cyber security as a genuine board-level agenda item, elevate the topic and the role, build it up as a genuine career elevator to inject raw talent — probably from business circles — and create the conditions for trust to rebuild around business security objectives driven top-down, instead of operational security objectives driven bottom-up.

It may lead to the emergence of CSO type of roles, returning historical CISO roles to their original technical purpose.

More than ever, this is crucial to drive real change across organisations made entirely dependent on digital services by the COVID crisis.

The Role
of the Board

#32 When True Innovation Consists of Doing Now What You Should Have Done Ten Years Ago

8 December 2016

Year after year, major surveys highlight low levels of cyber security maturity across large firms, and increasingly an even more worrying situation amongst smaller firms. The 2016 RSA Cyber Poverty index is a good example of that trend[1]. It truly paints a grim picture, but simply confirms findings that seem consistent across all large surveys – even if methodologies do vary.

Most of those surveys have another point in common: They are – in some form or another – organised or sponsored by heavyweights of the cyber security industry or large consultancy firms, who ultimately can be suspected of having an interest in accentuating negative traits in order to maximise their own sales.

But even if the results of those surveys have to be taken with great care for that reason, they do match an enormous amount of anecdotal evidence we come across in the field every day: Too many large firms – leaders in their field – are still struggling with fundamental basic principles of cyber security hygiene that have been regarded as good practice for 10 to 15 years, and for which technical solutions and organisational processes have been in existence for as long:

- Monitoring of basic network security events

- Timely deployment of security patches on servers and desktops

- Timely removal of user accounts

- Periodic revalidation of access levels with business units

It cannot be suggested that solving those problems is easy in large firms, and to a large extent the disappearance of the traditional business perimeter of the enterprise and the digital transformation of supply and value chains have made things even more complex.

---

1 RSA, Cyber Poverty Index, 2016

But those good practices have been relentlessly pushed forward by auditors and regulators, as well as Infosec professionals, for the best part of the last 10 to 15 years. Very large amounts of money have been spent with tech vendors on alleged solutions in those areas, so undoubtedly it is concerning that so little progress seems to have been made by so many firms in those domains over such a long period of time.

The most common root cause is a constant short-termist approach by senior management, focused solely on alleged "quick wins" or illusory technical solutions to audit or compliance problems, at the expense of the more complex process and governance transformation issues that would have driven real change but would have required a longer- term vision and approach.

The technology industry has done little to break those dynamics: In fact, it has been happily riding that wave for a long time, and the trend shows no signs of abating. It also has a long-standing tradition of re-inventing itself, and the cybersecurity sector is no exception. Most security vendors are now embracing emerging technologies such as Artificial Intelligence or Machine Learning, as well as more established platforms such as Big Data, and present as "innovative" Cloud-Based delivery models that in fact have been in existence – for some of them – for over 10 years.

They paint to their clients a situation where threats morph constantly, and therefore new tools are constantly required; and it may well be the case to some extent in some industries. But the harsh reality is that many of their clients don't have the basic processes in place that would enable them to take full advantage of such products, and at best they simply continue to buy those to put ticks in audit or compliance boxes, when it is not merely as a pet project for the CISO.

Many board members have woken up over the past few years to a situation they don't understand, being told all of a sudden that data breaches are simply a matter of time, often by the same people who have been telling them for years that everything was under control.

They need to realise that this is not just an external situation created by the acceleration of threats or some adverse economic or geopolitical outlook. Quite often, it is also the symptom of a serious internal problem rooted in decades of short-termism, adverse prioritisation of security matters and a complacent "tick-in-the-box" culture around audit and compliance.

We are coming to a point in many large firms where true "innovation" in the cyber security space does not consist in deploying the latest tools, but in going back to the governance drawing board, to look at long-term actions and remove the roadblocks that have prevented progress in the past, redesigning fundamental security processes across IT, the business and other support functions (such as HR etc...) in order to rebuild proper and functional operating models conceived to protect the organisation once and for all.

#33 Knee-Jerk Reactions to Data Breaches are damaging the case for Cyber Security

12 April 2016 – 19 May 2016

Cyber Security Transformation is not about implementing yet another technology product

Anybody who has spent a few years in InfoSec management has seen this happen: Following an internal near-miss or some high-profile security incident widely publicised in the media (such as the TalkTalk data breach in the UK), the same senior executives – who previously wouldn't bat an eyelid over information security issues – suddenly start panicking: Priorities shift. Immediate solutions are demanded. Money appears out of nowhere by the millions. Tech vendors are lined up. Some product is purchased that will allegedly fix everything. A box is checked, then normality returns.

Over the short-term, only the tech vendors win – shamelessly – in these scenarios.

The CISO – if there is one – loses ground in most cases. Unless they're just a technology hobbyist and they get another pet project to play with. Otherwise, they are likely to see their priorities turned upside down by the arrival of the new initiative and ongoing projects deprioritised in its favour.

This could be hugely demoralising for the CISO and their team who might have worked hard for years to get some projects started, that are now put on hold while other topics, that were repeatedly proposed and refused, are now pushed forward by the same executives who previously turned them down:

- It damages the credibility of senior management with the cyber security professionals.

- It makes life more difficult for the cyber security team in their day-to-day interaction with IT teams, as they are seen as constantly "moving the goal post".

- It perpetuates the wrong idea amongst IT communities that cyber security is just a topic you throw money at from time to time.

- In the long run, it alienates talent away from cyber security roles.

Cyber security products – broadly speaking – tend to do what they are supposed to do, so the chosen technology solution may provide a degree of protection to the organisation, but only if it gets implemented properly. And that's often the key issue. The product would have been selected in an emergency to plug a technical hole, not necessarily on the basis of the most thorough requirements analysis or market research:

It may not be suited to the company's environment (e.g. deploying internal security products while key IT assets are in the Cloud, or deploying Internet security products if your Internet footprint is limited).

There may be competing products or solutions already in place internally that could have been leveraged (e.g. in different geographies or business lines). Ignoring those alienates and demotivates part of the organisation and may deprive the initiative of invaluable field experience around the topic.

There may be considerable process issues when trying to embed the new product into legacy practices (e.g. around identity and access management or patch management) potentially leading to escalating costs, deployment limitations or project failure.

Overall, the knee-jerk decision may end-up being an expensive "tick-in-a-box" exercise that achieves very little in practice.

Even for tech vendors, the situation may not be ideal in the longer-term. As deployment fails or stalls due to technical issues, and value is limited by the lack of compatibility with people and processes, vendors may face dwindling revenue from subscriptions or cancellation of maintenance charges, which may damage business models or investors' confidence.

Senior executives need to understand the dynamics they create where they demand instant solutions to problems that are in reality rooted in decades of under-investment, adverse prioritisation or complacency. And the CIO and the CISO need to have the management gravitas and the backbone to stand up to the Board – with the right arguments – on those matters.

The harsh reality is that there can be no miracle solution – technical or otherwise – to such problems.

There may be a need for short-term tactical initiatives to demonstrate to the Board, shareholders or regulators that a new dynamic is being created around cyber security, but those have to be calibrated to the real maturity of the organisation around those matters, and the genuine threats it faces. As importantly, it must be accompanied by a thorough examination of the cultural roadblocks that have prevented progress in the past.

A genuine and lasting transformation around cyber security can only come from the removal of those, and from the definition of a long-term transformative vision for the function. A vision that must come from the top and resonate across the whole organisation, not just IT.

#34 The Six Questions the Board of Directors Needs to Ask[1]

7 August 2015 – 7 January 2016

From a cyber security perspective, the 2015 headlines have been dominated by a number of high profile data breaches: Sony, Ashley Madison, TalkTalk… Those have put the cyber security topic on the Board's agenda in many corporations and have also been drawing the attention of politicians.

Fundamentally, we believe that the Board of Directors needs to go back to basics on these matters: Time has now gone to continue approaching cyber security purely from a Risk perspective. Risk is ultimately about "things that may or may not happen". When it comes to cyber security, the Board should start from the premise that cyber-attacks are a matter of "when", not "if" – and should shift the focus towards understanding and managing what is actually getting done to protect the organisation.

The Board must not be allowed to believe that it needs to be involved simply because the cyber security topic is making headline news. The topic is making headline news because security breaches are occurring more and more often. This, in turn, is due to decades of complacency, neglect or short-termist "tick-in-the-box" practices around the Information and IT Security space. The problem is not new and those practices have resulted in low maturity and protection levels, that surveys keep highlighting year after year (for example in the 2015 RSA Cyber Poverty Index survey[2]).

In large organisations exhibiting such low levels of cyber security maturity, it would be misleading to allow the Board of Directors to believe it's a simple problem to fix – or that it simply requires the Board's supervision around a handful of key aspects. It is also misleading to allow the Board to believe in ready-made technical solutions or that throwing money at the problem will solve everything,

---

1   Originally published on Information Security Buzz; "Cyber Security: Board of Directors Need to ask the Real Questions", August 2015 (http://www.informationsecuritybuzz.com/articles/cyber-security-board-of-directors-need-to-ask-the-real-questions/)

2   RSA Cyber Security Poverty Index, 2015

as McKinsey & Co have recently highlighted in an article that echoes their 2014 findings for the World Economic Forum[1].

"Cyber Security is a high-stakes topic, so it is a CEO-level one", states the McKinsey article. However, the problem has some depth – and in many large organisations, where Cyber Security maturity levels are low, it could be rooted in 10 to 15 years of failure.

Understanding the true historical perspective of the problem and removing the roadblocks that have prevented progress in the past (people, resources, priorities… whatever they might be): These are the real issues which many organisations' Boards of Directors now need to confront and address.

Fig. 8: Cyber Security: Tthe 6 Questions the Board needs to ask

---

1   McKinsey & Co, « Repelling the Cyberattackers », 2015 (http://www.mckinsey.com/business-functions/digital-mckinsey/our-insights/repelling-the-cyberattackers)

1. What does it mean to us?

First of all, the Board must form an understanding of the nature of the cyber threats that might target the firm.

Cyber threats do not target all organisations in the same way – and some industry sectors are more exposed than others. Cyber security results from the application of proportionate controls to protect the business against the cyber threats it faces.

Understanding those threats is key to success and approaching the problem from a generic "one-size-fits-all" angle – or simply based on the content of media coverage – is dangerous and can lead to misguided judgements.

2. Who's in charge?

Having established its own understanding of the concepts, the first concern of the Board should be to ensure that cyber security responsibilities are clearly and unambiguously distributed across the organisation.

Cyber security should be formally part of the portfolio of a Board member, and accountability cascaded down (directly or indirectly) to an individual specifically tasked to make sure the business is, and remains, protected from cyber threats. This responsibility would lie with the CISO in many large organisations.

The reporting line of the CISO should be clear – and at a level allowing visibility, credibility and accountability across the organisation. The actual reporting line itself should be dictated by the priorities of the organisation, ahead of arbitrary separation of duties considerations.

The repartition of roles across the various lines of defence and across corporate silos should be clear. A sound Security Governance Framework and Target Operating Model should document those aspects across IT and beyond – into HR, Procurement, Legal, Corporate Communications and business units. They should cover, without complacency, the true geographical perimeter of the organisation and its dependency on third-parties where relevant.

3. What are we doing about it?

Having established that a sound Security Governance platform is in place across the business, the Board should ensure that key protective measures are (and remain) in place.

Starting with a sound appreciation of the threats the business faces (both internally and externally), a determination of the controls required to protect the business against such threats should naturally follow. These should be consolidated in a Cyber Security Controls Framework, specifically tailored to each organisation.

Relying on recognised generic industry frameworks and good practice catalogues instead is often preferred (or recommended by some vendors), but the approach has its pros and cons. On one hand, it is a sound way of making sure that all angles are covered; on the other, it could easily lead to over-engineering and over-spending – particularly for smaller firms.

Fundamentally, the Board should ensure that controls are proportionate to the threats the business faces – otherwise their deployment could be challenged or costs may escalate. The Board must look beyond which framework is actually being used, to focus on the way the controls it contains are effectively implemented across the organisation. Once again, it should also take into account the organisation's true geographical perimeter and its dependency on third-parties where relevant.

4. How exposed are we?

The Board should ask for periodic reports showing adherence of the organisation to its Cyber Security Controls Framework, and the primary focus should be on any deviations from this. Such deviations create opportunities for threats to target the business and cause harm, creating "Risk" – in the most classical sense of the word.

The Board should be concerned with any main issues – whether they're financial, organisational or technical – which are preventing the implementation of the Cyber Security Controls Framework, ensuring they remain updated on what is being done to address these.

The key threats should be those to which the firm is the most vulnerable (i.e. those against which it is the least protected). Once the key threats are identified, the Board should ensure that their organisation's incident response capability is regularly tested in those areas – if relevant.

The overall Cyber Risk Posture of the organisation should result from the analysis of deviations from an established Cyber Security Controls Framework.

5. How are we dealing with what is not under our direct control?

The Board should be concerned with 2 very different aspects in that space:

1. Dependency on Third-parties: The Board should be acutely concerned about dependency on third-parties, across the business and IT, as we have highlighted several times above. Many controls in the Cyber Security Controls Framework will have to be cascaded down to (and implemented by) a variety of external firms, but the organisation may have no actual means to enforce those – even if a breach in the other party environment could cause catastrophic damage to the business. As such, effective vendor risk management could be of critical importance for some organisations.

   The Board should start by building an understanding of the diversity and numbers of such vendors, and of those on which the business is most dependent. This must not be seen as a mere IT issue and it is key to approach it in terms of business processes. Following this, the Board should build an overview of those vendors' levels of adherence to the Cyber Security Controls Framework – or where relevant, of their unwillingness to cooperate with cyber security assessment efforts.

   Finally, the Board should ensure that unsatisfactory outcomes are being addressed – ensuring they remain updated on these matters. Board members also sitting on the Boards of some of the offending third-parties may want to take the matter into their own hands if and where they can.

Again, it is key to ensure that this is not turned into an IT matter – and that all business relationships are in scope.

2. Media & Political Interest: The Board should also be acutely concerned with the outcome of a cyber security breach spilling over into surrounding corporate areas – potentially contaminating their brand, customer trust, or shareholders' confidence.

   The dynamics of recent cases show that contamination often occurs as a result of aggressive media and political interest following breaches of privacy or service disruptions affecting the general public.

   While it is difficult to predict where media attention will be in relation to any particular service incident, the Board can build an understanding of the amount of sensitive personal data the organisation stores and processes. The Board should ensure it possesses a clear understanding of its legal duty of protection towards the privacy of its organisation's customers and staff – as well as the measures that are in place (or not) as part of the Cyber Security Controls Framework. The Board of international organisations should also be aware that those obligations may vary from country to country.

In all cases, the Board should ensure that the Security Governance Framework is active across all relevant corporate silos and reaches into all areas that may be involved in case of a breach – and that those interactions are regularly tested.

6. How do we protect our investment in cyber security?

The Board should be aware that cyber threats evolve constantly and that there is no silver bullet solution, technical or otherwise.

Ongoing protection can only come from a strong controls culture, embedded in the way the firm works. Such cultural shift could take time, particularly in organisations where cyber security maturity is low to start with, so taking a long-term view and sticking to it is key to success.

Ensuring that key personnel (the CISO and their team in many large organisations) remain in charge over the period is also key, and means they may have to consider their tenure over a 5 to 7 year horizon in many cases. Changing approach every 2 to 3 years every time a new CISO comes in is a recipe for disaster and could be very simply why so many large organisations still show such a low level of cyber security maturity.

The Board should also ensure that its direct involvement in cyber security matters is clear, unambiguous and widely publicised across the enterprise. The cyber security message from the Board should in turn be cascaded down across the organisation through regular management channels, and it is key for the staff to see that management (at their level) takes cyber security at heart. This type of bond is generally stronger, longer-lasting and cheaper to establish than any type of engagement through awareness development campaigns – which often miss the point entirely by being too tactical or too technical.

Finally, having examined all aspects listed above, the Board should consider the current level of cyber risk Insurance protection the firm holds (if any), and whether it provides adequate cover.

The Insurance question should come last, and the Board should consider adjusting cover if possible to match the findings highlighted by previous questions. The cyber risk insurance market is evolving fast, and products may be available today that were not available last time the Board inquired.

#35 Three factors marginalising the historical role of the CISO

24 May 2018

Is the CISO an outdated concept? And what to do about it?

The last SASIG meeting in London on 8th May 2018 examined the role and career of the CISO. It is hard to walk out of an event like this one not feeling that a number of things are seriously going round in circle in the security industry.

The reporting line of the CISO – on which I presented – is one of those topics which have been discussed constantly amongst security professionals for the best part of the last 15 years, but more generally, it felt like the role of the CISO was taken for granted as an established corporate concept.

That is far from being the case in my opinion, and as a matter of fact, the role does encompass very different responsibilities from an organisation to another and is rarely a true C-level function. Far from being reinforced by the constant avalanche of cyberattacks and data breaches of the past few years, it is being marginalised by three long-term trends:

1. The Cloud, Digital Transformation and the changing role of the CIO

Information assets are changing; they are being used in new ways across new media and across an increasingly complex dematerialised supply chain; the CIO has to share powers with CDOs and must deal with an increasing number of powerful service providers, and increased pressure from business units looking to gain a digital competitive advantage. Over time, the historical role of the CISO runs the risk of becoming the guardian of an increasingly empty shell surrounded by an increasingly complex web of supplier relationships, and little actual control over the real level of protection applied to sensitive information assets.

2. Resilience, Privacy and the consolidation of broader corporate concepts

Large scale cyber attacks over the past few years have put cyber risk on the Board's agenda, but "Information Security" – the traditional perimeter of the CISO – is often seen as only one aspect of a much bigger problem: The Board wants to see a full picture, encompassing the whole capability of the enterprise to sustain a cyber attack and recover from it. In larger firms, this "resilience" concept tends to lead to the emergence of broader enterprise security functions which push down the historical role of the CISO, as McKinsey & Co are rightly pointing out here[11].

One point McKinsey are missing – surprisingly – in this article is the importance privacy regulations are also playing – at least in Europe – in shaping up the board agenda around security. GDPR has been a big topic in many firms across the past 12 months. Tens of millions have been spent towards "compliance" in larger firms, and a good proportion of that went towards security-related measures, but many CISOs have failed to capitalise politically on the topic which has broadly been seen as a legal issue. The DPO roles and other "Chief Privacy Officer" functions which will emerge over the years to come from the implementation of the GDPR, are likely to create an additional corporate layer "breathing down the neck" of many CISOs and altering their historical ways of working.

3. Failure and the price to pay for the cyber security "lost decade"

For many senior executives, the actual role of the CISO – in its historical sense – is still a mystery. It is seen as complex and technical and it lacks a natural edge they could relate to. It feels like a "black art" always requiring more investments. At the same time, cyberattacks keep happening and often seem to point out to the absence of basic protective measures which could have been implemented years ago.

---

1   McKinsey & Co, "A new posture for cybersecurity in a networked world", March 2018 (https://www.mckinsey.com/business-functions/risk/our-insights/a-new-posture-for-cybersecurity-in-a-networked-world)

This "lost decade" of cyber security investments has damaged the profile of the CISO position in the eyes of many business leaders. And indeed many CISOs end up hopping from one job to another because they feel they can no longer achieve what they would like or are not being listened to.

So the role of the CISO in its historical technology-driven perception is not outdated yet, but it is under threat and losing ground.

The firms looking to reverse this trend need to act at three levels:

Elevate the personal profile of the CISO role by injecting real-life experience, managerial talent, personal gravitas and political acumen

Decouple the role from its historical technical profile and stop following blindly the misleading agenda of the technology industry; those historical aspects of the role can be separated into an "IT Security" function within the portfolio of the CIO or the CTO

Instead, turn the CISO function towards the new players in the field (CDO and DPO) and towards assisting the business units in all aspects of their digital transformation, dealing with third-parties and the associated evolution of the threat landscape

#36 On Cyber Security and Trust

4 January 2018

People simply trust other people

This excellent November piece from McKinsey on cyber security deserves a comment ("A Framework for Improving Cybersecurity discussions within Organizations" – Jason Choi / Harrison Lung / James Kaplan[11]).

The visualization of the "trust gaps" between the board, the business and IT and the firm, its suppliers and government is a very strong and synthetic way of representing where roadblocks emerge that prevent security strategies from being properly executed, therefore leaving organisations vulnerable to cyber threats.

We highlighted the importance of trust in a broader GRC context in an earlier article, and how dysfunctions breed when distrust sets in.

Of course, it is also true in the cyber security space: Let's take this opportunity to say this one more time: Firms protect their key assets from cyber threats through the actual deployment of security measures. It's not having a security strategy, or a plan in place that will protect your organisation but its actual implementation in the field, at the right levels and across the true perimeter of the enterprise, taking into account without complacency the true geographical footprint of the company and its true dependency on vendors and third-parties.

It is strategic execution that is key to protection from cyber threats, and therefore creating the conditions for execution to take place is paramount. Those conditions revolve around trust and closing the "trust gaps" identified in the McKinsey paper.

There are three key factors that will engineer trust and close those gaps:

Clarity of roles, responsibilities and objectives around cyber security from the board down internally and with third-parties

1   McKinsey & Co, "A framework for improving cybersecurity discussions within organizations", November 2017 (https://www.mckinsey.com/business-functions/digital-mckinsey/our-insights/a-framework-for-improving-cybersecurity-discussions-within-organizations)

Simplicity of language in the formulation of those roles, responsibilities and strategic objectives

And more importantly, Consistency over the right timeframes and the right budgetary allocations in terms of execution: Transformation in that space can be complex and take time because it often affects people, their culture and their real way of working. There is nothing more efficient at creating distrust on these matters than management changing direction or priorities every time something happens somewhere

It is also essential to reflect on the role and profile of the key people leading strategic execution, and in particular the CISO in the cyber security space.

Large firms are plagued by "ivory tower" head office functions which achieve very little in practice. Cyber security is no exception and is – all too often – one of those. Except that the stakes are getting higher and higher every year, and the time has come to create positive dynamics and break those deadlocks where they exist.

In most cases, navigating around the "trust gaps" and bridging them will require true leadership. The CISO job will never be a job for a junior technologist, an ex-auditor or a life-long consultant. It requires true political acumen and gravitas. Those attributes come with real-life field experience and an in-depth knowledge of the firm, its culture and its people that can only come from a substantial internal tenure, and a considerable managerial experience, in particular when it comes to influencing third-parties. Raising the profile of the CISO will often be key in many firms to efficiently bridge those "trust gaps".

Because in the end, people will be key to the strategic execution, and people simply trust other people. Internally and externally.

#37 A Cultural Revolution and a Matter of Corporate Social Responsibility for Tech Firms

10 March 2016

For years, many technology firms have treated security and privacy matters as an afterthought. It was at best a necessary evil related to regulations and compliance; at worst, something you would window-dress on the day in front of those few clients who would ask the question. It was seen as something boring and expensive, at odds with functionality and preventing innovation and agility.

Of course, with the convergence of IoT, Big Data and Cloud technologies, the cards are now dealt quite differently, and many tech companies – large and small – are starting to realize that they are going to have to adjust their mindset to survive, or make the most of the times ahead.

The convergence of those technology streams generates countless use cases in all industry sectors and has the genuine potential to transform our lives – and create trillions of dollars of economic value. But it also requires a type of hyper connectivity that multiplies attack surfaces exponentially and is highly vulnerable to cyber-threats. "Data" is currently treated by many tech firm as a free limitless commodity, and many of those firms talk about it as if it belonged to them and they could do whatever they like with it. But in practice, they acquire it most of the time through ludicrously one-sided terms of business which nobody reads, and from people – consumers, citizens – who have rights and expectations of privacy. It is only a matter of time until such practices start to be challenged.

The digital transformation of society will never realize its full potential as long as the trust of consumers and citizens is constantly being hammered by data breaches, cyber security incidents and ruthless data monetization by shameless vendors.

Technology vendors who want to stay in the game over the long term must take security and privacy seriously, and turn that into a competitive advantage for the generations of customers who share those values.

But it will be a massive cultural shift for many tech firms.

"Security by Design" and "Privacy by Design" principles have been established for a long while and they are still at the heart of what needs to be done to move forward:

Security features have to be treated, designed and tested as a proper product functionality embedded as early as possible in the way the product works – not as an add-on.

The respect of customers right to privacy has to be treated as a key business model parameter – not as something you will compromise on to make the numbers add up.

Whether the current generation of executives, investors, marketers & technologists running those firms is capable of understanding and delivering such shift in values is a key factor: The fundamental need for controls and the ethical treatment of customers at the heart of those principles is probably not something they were taught at business school.

But it is nevertheless the ability of those firms to embrace "Security by Design" and "Privacy by Design" concepts that will become the cornerstone of the digital transformation.

Fail to make the move and at best value creation will be reduced by several trillions (between 1 and 3 by 2020 according to McKinsey & Co for the 2014 World Economic Forum[1]); in practice, if it is the trust of the people that is irreparably damaged, it could be the dynamics of the entire digital transformation itself that might have to be re-considered.

With so much at stake, it is becoming a fundamental matter of corporate social responsibility for tech firms to take security and privacy values at heart.

---

1 McKinsey and Company, Risk and Responsibility in a hyperconnected world: Implications for Enterprises, 2014 (http://www.mckinsey.com/business-functions/digital-mckinsey/our-insights/risk-and-responsibility-in-a-hyperconnected-world-implications-for-enterprises)

#38 Cyber Security in the "When-Not-If" Era

14 March 2019

No longer just as an equation between risk appetite, compliance requirements and costs

The "When-Not-If" paradigm around cyber-attacks is changing the deal completely around cyber security.

Many large organisations now assume that breaches are simply inevitable, due to the inherent complexity of their business models and the multiplication of attack surfaces and attack vectors which comes with it.

This realisation changes fundamentally the dynamics around cyber security.

Historically, cyber security has always been seen as an equation between risk appetite, compliance requirements and costs. Compliance and costs were always the harder factors. Risk (difficult to measure and quantify) was always some form of adjustment variable.

Risk is about uncertainty. The "When-Not-If" paradigm brings certainty where doubt was previously allowed (or used to manipulate outcomes):

- Cyber-attacks WILL happen

- Sooner or later, regulators WILL step in

- They can now impose BUSINESS-THREATENING fines around the mishandling of personal data

- Media interest has never been higher around those matters: Business reputation and trust in a brand WILL be damaged by high-profile incidents

All the risk-based constructions which have been the foundations of many cyber security management practices are weakened as a result.

Compliance requirements remain (if anything, they are getting stronger as privacy regulators flex their muscles in Europe and the US) and costs cannot be ignored, but "are we spending enough?" has become a much more common question across the boardroom table, than "why do we need to spend so much?"

For CISOs, protecting the firm becomes an imperative: This is no longer about doing the minimum required to put the right ticks in compliance boxes, but very often a matter of genuine transformation: It forces them to work across corporate silos, look beyond the mere technology horizon (which is often their comfort zone), and also look beyond tactical firefighting (which often dominates their day-to-day).

Knowing what to do is often the easiest part: After all, good practices in the cyber security space have been well known for over a decade, and they still provide adequate protection against many threats – as long as they are properly implemented.

True cyber resilience can only come from real defence in depth, acting at preventative, detective, mitigative AND reactive levels, AND across the real breadth of the enterprise – functionally and geographically.

The "When-Not-If" paradigm will often bring the Board's attention and large resources onto cyber security, but with those will also come scrutiny and expectations: The challenge really becomes an execution and a leadership challenge for the CISO.

In large firms where a major overhaul of security practices is required, establishing a sound governance framework and operating model from the start will always be a key factor of long-term success for the CISO.

Equally important will be the need to put people and process first, and to identify the roadblocks which might have prevented progress in the past around cyber security matters.

Repeating the mistakes of the past would simply perpetuate the spiral of failure around security, as would an excessive or premature focus on tech solutions. There is no magical technology product which can fix in a few months what is rooted in decades of adverse prioritization, lip service and under investment.

The CISO must appreciate that and place all transformation efforts in the right perspective: Change takes time and relentless drive, and there may not be quick wins.

Managing expectations and staying the course will always be key pillars of any lasting cyber security transformation.

#39 What Cyber Resilience is Not About ...

25 April 2019

Cyber resilience must not be used to legitimise window-dressing practices around cyber security

Although the theme is gaining momentum, there is a certain amount of confusion around what cyber resilience really means for organisations.

For many, it is just another piece of consultant jargon: An abstract managerial concept with little real-life substance or meaning.

As a matter of fact, it is very real and rooted in the "When-Not-If" paradigm around cyber attacks which is changing completely the dynamics around cyber security in many firms.

At the heart of cyber resilience lies a real application of "defence in depth" principles which have been well established for decades: Acting at preventative, detective, mitigative AND reactive levels, AND across the real breadth of the enterprise – functionally and geographically. It is about the enterprise being enabled by the use of data and technology, whilst remaining protected from active threats.

It requires managerial and governance practices to be active across corporate silos and the supply chain (once again, functionally and geographically), and it cannot be dissociated from a broader approach to operational and corporate resilience.

It is hard to deliver at scale and presents many large organisations with significant cultural challenges. So the temptation is high for many to over simplify it and to focus only on alleged quick wins.

Of course, the "When-Not-If" paradigm implies that security breaches are unavoidable. But it does not represent a licence to ignore all protective, detective and mitigative measures to focus only on the reactive ones. This is the type of simplistic approach to "resilience" which may put a few ticks in audit or compliance boxes, but in the long term, can only aggravate security postures and lead to regulatory issues, in particular in the face of a worldwide tightening of regulations around the protection of personal data.

"Cyber resilience" cannot be limited to an annual desktop exercise with board members and corporate functions during which they simulate how to react to a cyber-attack, in order to minimise the impact on the share price, media coverage or the reactions of customers.

All those factors are important, but "cyber resilience" must not turn into an excuse to legitimise a top-down window-dressing culture around cyber security practices.

Corporate resilience is the ability of an organisation to continue operating in the face of disruptive events, and to return to normal operations over time. It implies a deep knowledge of operational processes, their integration and their inter-dependencies. It also implies a deep knowledge of the supply chain and its actors.

To operate efficiently in disrupted situations, it also requires a collaborative and positive culture, which needs to be created and fostered from the top down.

All this is even more acute in cyber resilience scenarios, due to their relative novelty, the speed at which the organisation often needs to react and the technical complexity which may be involved.

Instead of being treated as another box checking exercise and a quick win, cyber resilience must be embedded into the right corporate structures and used to channel a different culture from the top down around cyber security:

- A culture where cyber security (the need to protect the business from cyber threats) and the protection of individuals' privacy are not just matters of risk management or necessary evils imposed by compliance and regulations, but key business concepts and – increasingly –matters of competitive advantage and of corporate social responsibility.

- A culture which fosters the transversal nature of many security problems in large firms (looking across corporate silos, and certainly much beyond the mere technology horizon), because the security measures needed to protect the firm are transversal in nature: Their execution is the only factor that will protect the business and it requires transversal capabilities

- Finally, a culture rooted in transparency around security breaches because trust is the cornerstone of the digital economy and transparency is its foundation

#40 Cyber Security: Revisiting the Questions the Board Should Ask

22 August 2019

One Board member must be in charge and their pay package must ride on it

In 2015, in the wake of the TalkTalk data breach which made a massive impact in the UK media and even got politicians involved, we first explored the key questions the Board should ask in large firms around cyber security.

What a difference 4 years can make … At the time, our line of thought was very much on making the Board understand exposure to cyber threats and what was being done to counter them, especially across the supply chain as the concept of a hyper connected world bound by data and powered by emerging technologies was on the horizon.

At the time, the McKinsey Institute was estimating that emerging technologies could create up to USD 20 trillion of economic value, out of which cyber threats could destroy up to 3. Although we have seen no update on this research and its eventual accuracy, it cannot be denied that cyber-attacks have intensified and have been widely reported across the last 5 years – from Sony in 2015 to CapitalOne this year, with Equifax, British Airways and Marriott reporting breaches in the last 12 months alone, and not discounting the wide-spread Wannacry / NotPetya virus outbreak of 2017, which impacted badly industrial and logistics giants such as St Gobain or Maersk.

Equifax has now agreed to a USD 700M settlement for its 2017 data breach and the UK data privacy regulator is threatening British Airways and Marriott with nine figure fines under the UK equivalent of GDPR. So numbers are getting larger and larger and it is hard to imagine a Board member today in any large organisation who would be unaware of cyber threats.

Of course, priorities may vary in line with economic conditions or the general health of the business, but "cyber" in on the agenda of all Boards, and consistently rated as a top risk by many.

The last decade has undoubtedly be a decade of realisation for senior executives around cyber security: This is no longer about risk (things which may or may not happen) or compliance (boxes to tick and unnecessary bureaucracy): The "When-Not-If" paradigm has changed the game.

And with it the focus of the Board has shifted towards execution, very often in exchange of significant investments in cyber security – in particular where initial maturity levels were low.

This is no longer about understanding what's being done against cyber threats, it's about getting it done, and getting it done now.

So frankly, our 6 questions from 2015 now boil down to 2, in particular where a large programme of cyber security transformation is needed:

Who is in charge?

A Board member must take direct accountability and responsibility for the security transformation programme delivery. Period.

This is no longer about wheeling in the CISO twice a year. This is about getting clear and accurate reports on progress at each meeting, in return for the large investments consented.

So one Board member must carry the can. Preferably one closely associated with the operational challenges involved – not the Head of Risk or (with respect) the Head of HR…

This is not about knowing which head will roll at the next breach but giving the initiative the right profile: Any large-scale security transformation programme can only be complex and transversal. In global firms, the international aspects could add a considerable dimension to the task. Without the credible and visible backing of the most senior sponsor, chances of success are significantly diminished.

At the same time, the task must convey a degree of accountability, and must become a factor in determining the compensation level of the Board member in charge – in stock and in cash and with retrospect. The situation which has surrounded the ousted CEO of Equifax will not be tolerated much longer by consumers, citizens or politicians, and can only breed adverse sentiment against the corporate world and further regulation.

What are we doing about it?

Here, it is time to go back to the monitoring of good old-fashioned milestones against the deliverables of the programme of work.

What was meant to be done last month and did it get done? No need for convoluted "return-on-security-investments" discussions or fuzzy risk models.

Of course, the detailed tracking of achievement should be done downstream from the Board, in particular for large, complex or global programmes.

But the consolidated results should be clear, concise and factual and delivered in person by the Board member in charge.

Those 2 actions – personalisation and factualisation, underpinning a drive towards clarity and simplicity – will bring results over time, but here lies the main challenge for many Boards and their members:

Thinking over the mid to long-term and keeping steady orientations in the face of potentially changing business conditions is necessary to the success of any complex cyber transformation programmes because of their inherent transversal complexity (and also because in many cases, this is about catching up in a few years over 15 years of lip service or under investment).

The Board must be capable of driving a long-term vision for all this to work, even if "in the long-term, we're all dead" …

#41 Cyber Security: There are still Problems at the Top

11 February 2021

Only a cultural shift across the Boardroom can move the needle

The survey released by BT Security in January 2021 ("CISOs under the spotlight"[1]) is interesting, if only by the size of the population surveyed (over 7,000 people) and its triple focus on consumers, employees and business leaders.

But its findings are problematic, in particular in what they reveal of the attitude of senior executives towards cyber security, and the persistence of some problems at the top.

It starts well, with some stats broadly consistent with other surveys and anecdotal field evidence: 58% saying that improving data and network security has become more important to their organisation in the last year, and 76% rating their organisations as "good" or "excellent" at protecting itself from cyber threats.

But these stats are hard to reconcile with others in the report: On page 7, the mention that "fewer than one third of business leaders rate key components of their company's IT security as excellent" and that, broadly, they have "low confidence in the organisation's ability to deliver the fundamentals"; Also, on page 13, the statement that "fewer than half of executives and employees can put a name to their CISO"

Without a fuller access to the underlying dataset, it is hard to draw hard conclusions, beyond the fact that clearly an amount of confusion persists with business leaders around cyber security: How can you say that security is becoming more important and that your organisation is well protected, and at the same time, be unable to name your CISO??? And what does that tell us about the profile of the CISOs in those organisations???

---

1 See   https://www.globalservices.bt.com/en/insights/whitepapers/cisos-under-the-spotlight
and https://www.helpnetsecurity.com/2021/02/04/ciso-responsibilities/

Another aspect, typical of those surveys, is the emphasis on getting the security basics right, and the importance of awareness development with employees.

To truly move the needle on those matters, you need to go beyond the obvious and start confronting the real underlying issues. This is something on which we already commented last year, in relation to several reports from the World Economic Forum.

Of course, getting the basics right and training employees are essential pillars of any cyber security practice, but the real question remains: Why are we still here banging about it?

Good cyber security practices such as those mentioned in the BT survey – patching, access management, etc... – have been regarded as good practices for the best part of the last two decades, and large organisations which – collectively – would have spent tens or hundreds of millions on cyber security across that period, should not be in such poor state. Period.

The underlying causes of that failure are rooted in adverse prioritisation by the business, short-termism and internal politics. All factors pointing firmly towards problems of culture and governance at the top.

Until surveys such as this one, or the ones from the WEF we commented on last year, start tackling those issues, not much will move for good around cyber security.

The same, broadly, can be said around security awareness development. Of course, it's essential... but the "human firewall" has to start at the top of the organisation.

How can you expect staff to follow good practices and accept security constraints, if they see senior executives constantly allowed to skip the rules???

There is so much a CISO and their organisation can push horizontally across the business or bottom up, and without a clear and unambiguous endorsement from the top, the best cyber security awareness programme can quickly turn into an expensive box-checking exercise... The example must come consistently from the top, for any security awareness programme to stick and yield results.

So the CISOs are indeed "under the spotlights", but can they really "drive the reset" induced by the "speed and scale of the digital transformation triggered by the global pandemic"? (page 13)

In the current state of affairs, probably not.

The attitude senior executives have had towards security in most organisations over the past two decades has driven towards CISO roles a certain type of people. Most are technologists, consultants or auditors by background; very few come from true business roles.

So before the CISO can "drive the reset", it is the role itself that needs a reset. "Enterprises urgently need to elevate cybersecurity leadership" (page 13): On that point, the BT survey is spot on. But it is easier said than done.

Once again, this is something that has to come from the top and it may require a broadening of the traditional CISO portfolio towards continuity and privacy, effectively building up the role into an elevated CSO role able to reach across the organisation.

Such shift, supported at Board level and coupled with adequate compensation packages and career profiling, should attract a different type of executive and would drive change. This is the type of move we have been advocating since 2018 to address the challenges of the digital transformation and the increased demands on privacy compliance that came with GDPR.

But going back to the BT survey, to fix all this and get cyber security moving for good, you need to tackle the problem at Board level, not at CISO level.

It is only a cultural shift across the Boardroom which will move the needle.

#42 The 3 Biggest Mistakes the Board can Make around Cyber Security

25 February 2021

The protection of the business from cyber threats is something you need to grow, not something you can buy

The role of the Board in relation to cyber security is a topic we have visited several times since 2015, first in the wake of the TalkTalk data breach in the UK, then in 2019 following the WannaCry and NotPeyta outbreaks and data breaches at BA, Marriott and Equifax amongst others. This is also a topic we have been researching with techUK, and that collaboration resulted in the start of their Cyber People series and the production of the "CISO at the C-Suite" report at the end of 2020.

Overall, although the topic of cyber security is now definitely on the board's agenda in most organisations, it is rarely a fixed item. More often than not, it makes appearances at the request of the Audit & Risk Committee or after a question from a non-executive director, or – worse – in response to a security incident or a near-miss.

All this hides a pattern of recurrent cultural and governance attitudes which could be hindering cyber security more than enabling it.

There are 3 big mistakes the Board needs to avoid to promote cyber security and prevent breaches.

1. Downgrading it: "We have bigger fishes to fry..."

Of course, each organisation is different and the COVID crisis is affecting each differently – from those nearing collapse, to those which are booming.

But pretending that the protection of the business from cyber threats is not a relevant board topic now borders on negligence and is certainly a matter of poor governance which non-executive directors have a duty to pick up.

Cyber attacks are in the news every week and have been the direct cause of millions in direct losses and hundreds of millions in lost revenues in many large organisations across almost all industry sectors.

Data privacy regulators have suffered setbacks in 2020: They have been forced to adjust down some of their fines (BA, Marriott), and we have also seen a first successful challenge in Austria leading to a multi-million fine being overturned (EUR 18M for Austrian Post). Nevertheless, fines are now reaching the millions or tens of millions regularly; still very far from the 4% of global turnover allowed under the GDPR, but the upwards trend is clear as DLA Piper highlighted in their 2021 GDPR survey, and those number should register on the radar of most boards.

Finally, the COVID crisis has made most businesses heavily dependent on digital services, the stability of which is built on sound cyber security practices, in-house and across the supply chain.

Cyber security has become as pillar of the "new normal" and even more than before, should be a regular board agenda, clearly visible in the portfolio of one member who should have part of their remuneration linked to it (should remuneration practices allow). As stated above, this is fast becoming a plain matter of good governance.

2. Seeing it as an IT problem: "IT is dealing with this…"

This is a dangerous stance at a number of levels.

First, cyber security has never been a purely technological matter. The protection of the business from cyber threats has always required concerted action at people, process and technology level across the organisation.

Reducing it to a tech matter downgrades the subject, and as a result the calibre of talent it attracts. In large organisations – which are intrinsically territorial and political – it has led for decades to an endemic failure to address cross-silo issues, for example around identity or vendor risk management – in spite of the millions spent on those matters with tech vendors and consultants.

So it should not be left to the CIO to deal with, unless their profile is sufficiently elevated within the organisation.

In the past, we have advocated alternative organisational models to address the challenges of the digital transformation and the necessary reinforcement of practices around data privacy in the wake of the GDPR. They remain current, and of course are not meant to replace "three-lines-of-defence" type of models.

But here again, caution should prevail. It is easy – in particular in large firms – to over-engineer the three lines of defence and to build monstrous and inefficient control models. The three lines of defence can only work on trust, and must bring visible value to each part of the control organisation to avoid creating a culture of suspicion and regulatory window-dressing.

3. Throwing money at it: "How much do we need to spend to get this fixed?"

The protection of the business from cyber threats is something you need to grow, not something you can buy – in spite of what countless tech vendors and consultants would like you to believe.

As a matter of fact, most of the breached organisations of the past few years (BA, Marriott, Equifax, Travelex etc… the list is long…) would have spent collectively tens or hundreds of millions on cyber security products over the last decades…

Where cyber security maturity is low and profound transformation is required, simply throwing money at the problem is rarely the answer.

Of course, investments will be required, but the real silver bullets are to be found in corporate culture and governance, and in the true embedding of business protection values in the corporate purpose: Something which needs to start at the top of the organisation through visible and credible board ownership of those issues, and cascade down through middle management, relayed by incentives and remuneration schemes.

This is more challenging than doing ad-hoc pen tests but it is the only way to lasting long-term success.

The Fabric
of a Successful
Security Practice

#43 The Key Steps Towards a Successful InfoSec Practice[1]

30 June 2015 – 3 September 2015

This series deconstructs eight commonly held views on Information Security that CIOs would have encountered, and highlights the key Governance and Leadership rules CIOs and CISOs should follow to build and deliver a successful Information Security practice.

1. Think of Information Security as a Control function and not as a Support function

Information Security within a large organisation is often simplistically seen as a support function, and, as such, many stakeholders expect it to help streamline or 'enable' the business. The reality is, Information Security needs to be seen as a control function – and rules (that may be perceived as restrictive) are a necessary part of ensuring its effectiveness. CISOs must have the management skills to effectively communicate the threats facing the information assets to all stakeholders across the business – and they must get everyone on the same page when it comes to ensuring the appropriate controls are put in place to protect these assets.

2. Create a sense of reality around the threats and do not focus only on IT aspects

A commonly held view among Information Security communities is that businesses don't care enough about Information Security – and decisions are often made from a convenience or cost avoidance perspective. However, a disproportionate focus on technical details and IT issues by the security teams themselves is often to blame for the disengagement with the subject. It's down to the CISO to effectively communicate to the business the real threats faced by information assets, how this could translate into real consequences across the organisation – and how protective controls can prevent

---

1 Originally published on the Broadgate Consultants blog; "The CIO guide to a successful Information Security practice", June 2015 (http://www.broadgateconsultants.com/blog/2015/06/30/the-cio-guide-to-a-successful-information-security-practice/)

this from happening. If the level of Risk (resulting from the presence or absence of controls) is presented in a language that the businesses can understand, the CISO will build a meaningful dialogue with them that should drive the right decisions.

3. Focus resources on the proper implementation of key Controls and sell success

It's often believed that Information Security is a chronically underfunded practice, and budgetary limitations are a barrier to its success. However, research by the World Economic Forum[1] has shown that many large organisations in fact spend more than 3% of their total IT budgets on cyber security. Despite this, few have reached an acceptable level of cyber security maturity. Instead of requesting budgets to fund new technical initiatives, CISOs should tilt the magnifying glass and focus the resources they do have on the proper implementation of key controls – which have been mapped for a long time and alone can be highly successful in preventing most cyber attacks. Implementing demonstrable controls will give the business confidence that real protective measures are being put in place and that the spend is justified.

4. Pin tactical initiatives against a long-term Information Security roadmap

Within Information Security communities, the CISO is frequently regarded as a 'firefighter', working mostly in a reactive manner around cyber security incidents and attacks. This approach is often further fuelled by management's short-term obsession with audit and compliance issues. While reacting to breaches or acting on regulatory demands will always remain a priority, especially as cyber threats continue to evolve and regulation increases, the key focus should be on addressing the root cause of the underlying problems. The CISO must pin tactical initiatives against the backdrop of a long term transformative Information Security roadmap and think beyond mere technical and tactical solutions. But to be truly successful, the CISO must also have the gravitas to influence lasting change and the personal skills to drive security transformation.

---

1 World Economic Forum, « Risk and Responsibility in a Hyper-connected world », 2014 (with McKinsey & Co)

5. Assign Information Security Responsibilities and Accountabilities

Countless security awareness programmes follow the train of thought that Information Security is everyone's business – across the organisation. While it's true that everyone in an organisation can do something at their level to protect the business against threats, it cannot be 'everyone's responsibility' – as this attitude can quickly derive towards becoming 'nobody's responsibility'. The CIO must ensure that the CISO is accountable for ensuring that the appropriate controls are in place across the organisation, backed by a sound Information Security Governance Framework. They must ensure that accountabilities and responsibilities are cascaded down to all relevant stakeholders across all silos (e.g. HR, Legal, Business units, third-parties etc.).

6. Operate Information Security as a cross-silo practice and not just as a technical discipline

Information Security practice is regularly considered a purely technical discipline. However, information exists in both digital and physical forms and more importantly – is constantly manipulated by people during the business day. While technology should undoubtedly play a strong role, in many industries, a stronger focus on the other elements of Information Security is often required. In order to implement an effective Information Security practice, CISOs need to establish a controls based mind-set across all silos of their organisation.

7. Operate Information Security as an ongoing structured practice and not just a series of technical projects

Information Security practitioners always seem busy with technical projects. In fact, Information Security should be there to provide continuous and long-term protection to the business. Therefore, it should not be approached just as a series of tactical projects with a set start date, end date and check-list of deliverables. All technical projects and tactical initiatives within an organisation's Information Security practice should be seen as forming part of a structured practice and aligned with a long term Information Security strategic roadmap – aiming to achieve an Information Security vision and deliver lasting change across the organisation.

8. Operate Information Security to focus on People and Process supported by Technology, not just the implementation of the latest Technical Products

In order to 'keep up with the hackers' as technology evolves and cyber-attacks become increasingly more advanced, many believe that business protection is derived primarily from the implementation of the latest technical products and solutions. While it can be tempting to believe that the latest technology products are going to be the 'silver bullet' needed to keep the business safe, in reality there's often more to consider. It's critical that the Information Security practice addresses any weaknesses in the organisation's functional structure (people and processes), before turning to technical products as potential solutions.

#44 Think of Information Security as a Control function and not as a Support function

7 May 2015

There is a commonly held view across Information Security communities that Information Security should be an "enabler" to the business. This is simply the wrong debate and one that CIOs and CISOs must avoid: Information Security results from the application of controls around Information to protect the business from the threats it faces.

The "Security as an enabler" cliché is often used in contexts where Information Security functions have historically promoted approaches perceived by business or IT communities as arbitrary and negative (i.e. "disabling"). But it is a cliché also applied broadly to many Support functions in a large organisation (IT, HR, Procurement as an "enabler" etc.). It simply means that the business expects Support functions to make it work better and not to impose arbitrary or bureaucratic barriers.

But Information Security is more complex than that and it cannot be seen just as a Support function, ensuring that business processes run safely. It needs to be a Control function, mandating protective measures and ensuring that they are implemented. It is there to protect the business from real and active threats – this is no more (or less) enabling than roofs over heads or locks on doors. And saying no to some individuals is sometimes necessary to protect the business as a whole.

The CISO must have the personal, professional and political gravitas to communicate effectively the reality and seriousness of the threats to all business stakeholders. The need for protection should follow as a natural consequence. Proportionality and common sense should prevail throughout (i.e. ensuring the adequacy of controls in proportion to the threats), and all decisions about Controls (including budgetary and financial decisions) should be made in the context of a structured Information Security Governance model.

#45 Create a sense of reality around the threats and do not focus only on IT aspects

14 May 2015

Another commonly held view across Information Security communities is that the business doesn't really care about Information Security. Businesses often end up making decisions about Controls from a convenience or cost avoidance perspective, without really understanding the Information Security context and the Risk.

Very often, it is not that the business does not understand the need to protect Information – but that the CISOs and their teams focus too much on the technical details. At best, it perpetuates the bad practice of treating Information Security as a mere IT discipline. At worst, it damages relationships as the business is just not interested in this level of detail.

Risk is a consequence of the absence or deficiency of controls. The business can only manage Risk on the basis of a clear understanding of the threats it faces – and the real Controls that are in place to protect it from those threats. Controls work in layers, with some counteracting the absence of others.

It is down to the CISO to communicate this to the business, creating a strong sense of reality around the nature of the threats the business faces and the natural need for protective controls. In turn, the CISO should ensure the proportionality of controls (in relation to the threats), and the business should drive action as it sees fit (and understand the consequences).

To be successful in building up this dialogue, CISOs will have to look beyond pure IT Security matters to talk to the business in management terms and in terms of business processes supported by technical solutions (not the other way round).

The business will generally understand if spoken to in its own language. Breaking silos across business, IT and other communities (HR, Legal, Insurance etc.) to deliver real, effective and efficient Controls platforms and ongoing support around those is key to success for CISOs.

But, ultimately Risk can only be signed off through the right Governance mechanisms once all relevant aspects have been taken into account and not on a "piecemeal" basis. If the threats faced by the business are real, and the mandated controls are proportionate, a technical "waiver" (possibly poorly understood) signed off by one business stakeholder does not remove any risk. It simply creates a Controls gap that can be exploited and exposes the organisation. It must be recorded, regularly reviewed and where relevant, escalated as part of a structured Information Security Governance model.

Some Information Security practices have developed over time a proper "cottage industry" around such "waivers". This is not right and should not be endorsed by auditors and regulators as a valid risk management mechanism on its own.

If the business is constantly challenging the proportionality of the mandated controls or the real nature of the threats, then the CISO must look with great care at the structure of their own policies and practices and consider the necessary adjustments.

In all cases, a clear Information Security Governance framework should be in place – assigning roles, responsibilities and accountabilities for all stakeholders across business, IT and all relevant communities. This allows a meaningful dialogue to take place around those issues and the right decisions to be made at the right level, including any budgetary or financial considerations – without complacency (i.e. taking into account the true geographical perimeter of the business and all relevant partners and suppliers).

#46 Focus resources on the proper implementation of key Controls and sell success

21 May 2015

Another commonly held view across Information Security communities is that Information Security is critically and chronically under-funded, and that obtaining the budgetary allocations it deserves is always difficult.

In fact, many large organisations (> $5B Market Caps) claim to spend in excess of 3% of their total IT spend on cyber security[1], and on the whole – large firms have invested very significant amounts over time in Information Security.

Most of them would have had Information Security practices in operation for years, but according to the same report – in spite of the amounts invested, 79% have not yet achieved a recognisable level of cyber security maturity. This was highlighted in our February 2015 analysis of the World Economic Forum report published on computing.co.uk[2].

The business appetite for more investment is frequently limited by the absence of tangible results, as CISOs and their teams constantly ask for more technical resources to drive new technical initiatives. However, properly implemented essential controls can actually prevent approximately 80% of cyber-attacks – according to the UK GCHQ[3].

What Information Security teams critically need, is to focus their significant resources (budget and people) towards the real, proper and demonstrable implementation of those key controls. Focusing on People and Process as well as Technology, rather than constantly following the latest technology trends, can prevent breaches.

---

1 World Economic Forum, « Risk and Responsibility in a Hyper-connected world », 2014 (with McKinsey & Co)

2 How to achieve effective cyber security in a hyperconnected world, February 2015 (https://www.computing.co.uk/ctg/opinion/2396800/how-to-achieve-effective-cyber-security-in-a-hyperconnected-world)

3 Institute of Directors "Big Picture"; "Countering Cyber Threats to Business", Spring 2013

This is about vision, priorities and results – not just resources. The business will generally give budget if they have the confidence that real protective measures will be delivered. CIOs and CISOs must sell success internally against the backdrop of a clear long-term Information Security vision and within the context of a clear Information Security Governance model.

It should be natural for the business to want to protect itself against real and active threats, and to give resources to a person and a team that can articulate a clear vision in that respect – creating a sense of direction, and inspiring confidence that things will get done.

#47 Pin tactical initiatives against a long-term Information Security roadmap

28 May 2015

Another commonly held view across Information Security communities is that the CISO can only be a fire fighter because of the virulence of cyber threats and the endemic short-termist obsession of Management with audit and compliance issues.

As mentioned in the previous article in this series, 79% of large organisations have not yet achieved any recognisable level of cyber security maturity – and cyber threats are continuing to evolve at a faster and faster pace. So it is understandable that many organisations face immediate problems stemming from incidents or near-misses.

Those must be always addressed and will always require a degree of priority, but successful CISOs must look beyond this and address the root causes of these problems. They must pin those tactical initiatives against the backdrop of a long term transformative Information Security roadmap and think beyond mere technical solutions to cover all relevant People and Process aspects as well.

Failure to achieve this, and reliance on short-term audit or compliance-driven objectives without addressing the underlying cultural or structural issues that have created problems to start with, can only perpetuate an endless project-driven cycle of fire-fighting and breed bad practices.

In most large organisations where current cyber security levels are low, the role of the CISO must be one of a Change Agent – and the CISO must be prepared to stay in charge for the time it will take for real change to take roots. In most large organisations, this will involve (at least) an initial transformation cycle of several years, followed by a consolidation cycle of several years. The CISO must be incentivised to keep their position for that long. Governance and culture are key to driving lasting change and any change momentum can be devastated by the untimely withdrawal of key personnel.

Lasting change can only stem from a clear long-term Information Security vision and be built around a clear Information Security governance model. This should assign roles, responsibilities and accountabilities to all stakeholders across the business, IT and all relevant communities – without complacency (i.e. taking into account the true geographical perimeter of the business and all relevant partners and suppliers).

A clear long-term Information Security roadmap should also allow CIOs and CISOs to fend off arbitrary audit observations and remain in control of their own priorities.

The CISO must have the right blend of technical and Management experience to achieve this, coupled with personal gravitas and political acumen to drive change. These are attributes of seniority that are fairly rare and finding the right profile is key to success.

#48 Assign Information Security Responsibilities and Accountabilities

4 June 2015

Another commonly held view across Information Security communities is that Information Security needs to be everybody's responsibility.

This is the cliché against which countless Security awareness development programmes have been justified – and while there is an element of truth in the fact that each employee can do something at their level to protect the organisation against threats, this is true across the board and is not specific to Information threats.

In practice, most awareness programmes are missing the point by focusing excessively on a technical message to the detriment of the emotional message. Employees will only change their attitudes to protect the organisation if they care about it to start with. To be effective over the long-term, awareness programmes should insist primarily on those emotional aspects – in a way similar to public campaigns targeted at anti-alcohol abuse or road safety have been structured, and develop the protective bond between the employee and the company. And measuring progress should be built-in from the start, through the definition of key indicators and internal focus groups or polling methods.

Of course, this is far more complex (and costly) than distributing leaflets or mouse mats – and it would force the CISO to work across silos with HR and other corporate functions. Results are hard to predict, let alone return on investment, and can only be rooted in the corporate culture of each organisation. While well-designed long-term awareness programmes can be an element in the machinery that drives change, when structured around an opportunistic technical angle – and without metrics to measure progress – they can be a catastrophic waste of money.

The CIO must not look at those as any kind of "silver bullet" to deliver change in the Security space, even in very large organisations where it seems nothing else could be practically delivered on a global scale due to complex geographical or business spread (and in actuality those very aspects could make awareness programmes even more difficult to drive).

Driving change in the Information Security space is complex and takes time. It can only stem from a clear long-term vision and from the clear assignment of accountabilities, responsibilities and reporting lines at the top – backed by the right HR provisions in terms of performance management and rewards for key actors.

Information Security cannot be just "everybody's responsibility". Over time it may just become "nobody's responsibility". It needs to be "somebody's responsibility" and that person can only be the CISO.

The CIO must ensure that the CISO is clearly and unambiguously accountable for ensuring that the right controls are in place across the organisation, backed by an Information Security Governance Framework that ensures that accountabilities and responsibilities are cascaded down to all relevant stakeholders.

#49 Operate Information Security as a cross-silo practice and not just as a technical discipline

11 June 2015 [Author – Neil Cordell]

Another commonly held view across Information Security communities is that Information Security needs to be primarily a technical discipline.

At face value, this view doesn't make sense because Information exists in both physical and digital forms – and, more importantly, it is constantly manipulated by people as part of business processes. Whilst most business processes are increasingly dependent on technology, this is not true for all of them (across industries) and certain ones will not benefit greatly from the use of technology.

The role of the CISO will always need to have a technical dimension – as a large amount of information is processed through technology and threats often target technology directly. The CISO must understand the technical context to a sufficient degree in order to remain credible when facing IT stakeholders.

However, Information must be protected at physical, functional and digital levels – and a successful Information Security practice needs to operate across the various silos in the organisation in order to protect the business. Therefore, the CISO will also need to have a significant understanding of the business so that they can communicate with the business leaders in their own language. It is essential that the CISO builds trust in the Information Security practice with all of the stakeholders (Business, IT, HR, Legal, Compliance, etc.).

Consequently, in most large organisations, the day-to-day activities of the CISO will be geared primarily towards management and governance – and the CISO absolutely needs to have the management experience, personal gravitas and political acumen to influence across the business and IT. A clear long-term vision, governance and target operating model around Information Security is the only way to make CISOs successful in the long-term and enable them to generate and maintain change momentum.

To be successful in Information Security requires a controls based mind-set which reaches into all aspects of an organisation in order to appropriately protect the business. This can only be done by looking beyond the technical aspects and cutting across all the traditional silos within the organisation.

#50 Operate Information Security as an ongoing structured practice and not just a series of technical projects

18 June 2015 [Author – Neil Cordell]

Another commonly held view across Information Security communities is that an Information Security practice needs to drive technical projects.

In the previous article, it was highlighted that Information Security needs to be a cross-silo practice rather than a purely technical discipline. The necessary controls around Information are required to protect the business from the threats it faces and have to form part of that mind-set, instead of being seen as a necessary evil or an occupational hazard. Some will be delivered through IT platforms and others through physical measures, functional measures within business processes, or managerial methods.

Therefore, it does not make sense to consider Information Security just as a series of technical projects. One of the key attributes of a project is that it has a start date and an end date with a number of clearly defined deliverables. If Information Security is merely structured as a series of projects then it will be focused on the delivery of specific items rather than an ongoing structured practice which provides continuous protection to the business.

Technical projects must form part of a strategic roadmap – required to achieve an Information Security vision which will deliver lasting change to both the business and the Information Security practice. Otherwise, there can be no guarantee that these projects will be properly organised or joined up.

There is no magical tool or method to achieve that, and it is dangerous to believe that a technical approach alone can deliver it.

Ultimately, a successful Information Security practice needs to be an ongoing practice, structured around a clear Target Operating Model that architects all activities performed across the function. The CISO has to be the catalyst to make it happen and deliver cost-effective protection to the business. The CISO must drive a Security mind-set across the firm and cannot be just another IT project manager.

#51 Operate Information Security to focus on People and Process supported by Technology, not just the implementation of the latest Technical Products

25 June 2015 [Author – Neil Cordell]

Another commonly held view across Information Security communities is that, given the current level of cyber threats, business protection is primarily driven by the implementation of the latest technical Information Security products (in order to "keep up with the hackers").

Given the complexity of the cyber landscape – and the speed at which both technologies and the related threats are evolving – it is clear that technical Information Security products are essential to assisting in the protection of information assets. However, it is often easy to forget that information assets do not have a single digital dimension and that, ultimately, it is the combination of digital controls and people's actions – coupled with the right physical and functional processes – that form the strongest line of defence.

Therefore, to create an effective protection framework for information assets, it is critical for solution architecture and design to focus on people, process, and a clear definition of roles and responsibilities amongst all stakeholders – before looking for specific technical Information Security products.

It is all too easy to believe that the latest Information Security technology is always a "silver bullet" to protect the business. The key to not falling into this trap is to properly understand the threats that you are trying to protect your business against and to focus always on the most appropriate controls to be implemented. What is it a particular new line of technology will achieve? Can it be practically deployed across the organisation? And will it actually improve the protection of the business, or is it just somebody's "pet project"? Not all controls need to be technical in nature and sometimes procedural controls will be both more effective and efficient to implement.

Technology vendors are all too keen to sell their products and highlight the benefits that may be derived – but this often ignores the complexities of actually implementing the product across the complete scope of a large organisation.

This all too frequently leads to a situation where a product only ever gets partially implemented and can have a number of potentially damaging consequences:

The business may be unaware that the complete implementation has failed so will falsely believe that it is better protected than it actually is.

When made aware (and in particular if this is a recurring event), the business may question the value of the Information Security function which could erode the CISO's credibility or their ability to secure future budgets.

The Information Security team is likely to be frustrated that they have not completed the implementation and don't have visibility or control across the entire organisation.

The vendor is unlikely to be happy in the longer term because the customer may question recurring charges or the purchase of additional products.

Always following the latest Information Security technical trends can be dangerous for CISOs. It may assist in putting ticks in audit and compliance boxes but it also detracts resources from the implementation of essential controls. As mentioned in an earlier article in this series, these essential controls can prevent approximately 80% of cyber-attacks according to the UK GCHQ. Technical solutions have existed for many years to enable the essential controls – and the CISO's priority must be to ensure that they are properly put in place in support of the right processes.

Making it
Work in
Real Life

#52 Cyber Security Transformation is Rooted in Governance and Culture; not Technology

23 February 2016 – 14 April 2016 [with Vincent Viers]

Compliance and audit-oriented "tick-in-the-box" practices are still underpinning many InfoSec strategies. Huge sums of money are being spent on supposedly "one-size fits all" reactive solutions to one-off threats. However, such a firefighter mentality is at odds with the holistic, preventive protection that an efficient 21st century InfoSec strategy requires.

Cyber threats have become increasingly salient for most organisations, with potentially fatal consequences in terms of operations, finance and reputation. The board must realise the growing ubiquity of such threats—and the hard, cold fact that cyber-attacks are no longer a matter of "if" but a matter of "when".

This is not just a technology problem

Your organisation forms the most efficient shield against potential threats, and as such a transition towards an effective InfoSec Governance is the only way ahead. A clear, simple and consistent security mindset must be embedded at every level of the organisation. For many large organisations, this is no longer a matter of awareness development, but a profound matter of cultural change.

Rome was not built in a day. Neither will a lasting InfoSec culture.

As with any organisational change, it will always be a medium to long term journey.

For most of the Roman Empire's glory, the protection of the city of Rome was deemed a secondary issue which could be addressed on an ad-hoc basis with interventions by the Roman Army. It took the Romans more than 300 years, and the pressure of a growing crisis due to barbarian threats, to finally decide to build the Aurelian Walls as a consistent and lasting security strategy for their city. They took 4 years to build, but they protected the city for almost 2 centuries.

As Cyber security transformation experts, we feel a lesson can be drawn from history. Most organisations' current approach to InfoSec is, in many regards, very similar to that of overconfident Roman emperors—short-term oriented, overly expensive, and inefficient in the face of growing threats. Good practices have existed for decades and will go a long way to protect against those threats, but they need to be in place.

In that respect, for many large organisations, driving cyber security change starts by looking back and removing the roadblocks that have prevented action in the past. All of those – under investment, adverse prioritisation, complacency – do challenge governance and cultural practices up to Board level. Addressing them is a complex management exercise, and definitely not an IT matter.

#53 Getting real business value out of cyber security assessments

14 January 2016

7 real-life tips for cyber security practitioners and senior executives who want to look beyond technical "box-checking" approaches

Cyber security assessments can be conducted for a variety of reasons. More often than not, in response to regulatory concerns, third-party requests or executive management questions following a widely publicised data breach (the "could-it-happen-to-us?" type of scenario).

They are also often ordered by incoming senior executives trying to understand the true nature of the security landscape around them.

Key – in this context – is to create an assessment dynamic that will produce reliable actionable results, instead of a mere "tick-in-the-box" exercise that middle-management could manipulate to justify existing IT projects or the status-quo.

There are countless software assessment tools that can be used in that space, but it is key to start from governance, process and methodology, before looking for the right automation tool.

The most common mistake with cyber security assessments – in particular in large organisations – is to design an assessment practice around the capabilities of a software tool. Business value will not come directly from any software functionality, but from the assessment's relevance, the true engagement of key stakeholders and their trust in the validity of the results.

Relevance will come from understanding the legacy context in which the assessment is rooted. Engagement and trust will come out of honesty, competence, transparency and the independence of the assessors from any legacy situation.

In order to generate a true transformational dynamic out of this, a number of key management rules have to be followed.

Fig. 9: The Cybersecurity Assessment Cycle

1. Cyber Security Assessments must start from the start: What are the cyber threats the organisation faces?

The assessment practitioners should start by "doing their homework" instead of relying on generic ready-made statements, and identify threats agents, attack vectors and attack surfaces in the actual context of the organisation being assessed.

They should look without complacency at the true geographical footprint of the business and its dependency on third-parties, as well as industry dynamics around threats & recent attacks.

On that basis, they must assemble a number of compelling war stories to open the eyes of executive management (if necessary) on the real nature of the cyber threats their business is facing.

2. Understand the existing organisation and its culture to build a clear governance framework surrounding the assessment from the start

Getting the governance context right from the start is also fundamental to engineer acceptance of the assessment results and – ultimately – drive corrective action by the right stakeholders at the right level.

The assessment sponsors must be clearly identified: The assessment practitioners must understand without ambiguity who they are working for and what the sponsors objectives are, how the assessment's results are going to be used (e.g. reporting into risk and compliance or audit committees), and by whom, for what purpose, and at which frequency. The internal culture surrounding "controls" at large must also be understood.

The purpose and context of the exercise must be clear: Assessing Compliance? (against what?) Assessing Risk? (what does that mean?) Assessing Maturity? (according to which model?) Is this going to be a "one-off" or a periodic exercise? What are the timeframes involved?

The actual scope of the exercise and the key stakeholders must be clearly identified: Who is in charge of what? Is there one specific individual identified as being in charge of cyber security? Practitioners must understand as much as possible the roles – past and present – of the various parties in relation to the existing cyber security posture of the organisation being assessed, and their reporting lines. Again, they must not underestimate the true geographical footprint of the business and its dependency on third-parties.

On the basis of the analysis detailed above, a clear steering committee format, membership and meeting schedule should be defined and signed off with all parties to oversee the assessment exercise over the required timeframes (multiple committees may be required at different levels for large organisations; equally, existing committee structures may be re-used where relevant).

3. Assembling the assessment team: Balance experience with common sense and inquisitiveness

The team can be structured around internal resources or rely on external consultants, but in all cases, it must be totally independent from the pre-existing cyber security organisation and any legacy situation or arrangement.

Assessment team members must have a degree of knowledge of the cyber security field, but they do not need to be all subject-matter experts and they must not be all technologists.

They must have enough experience to spot nonsense, understand what to challenge and where to stop. At the same time, they need to have the inquisitiveness to dig in the right areas or look behind the curtains.

Fundamentally, they must be empathetic and able to build trust with stakeholders by showing them they understand their constraints.

4. Assembling the assessment checklist: Firmly root your assessment in existing material – good or bad; Do not trust ready-made checklists

Practitioners must start from existing internal material in terms of policies, procedures and guidelines to build their assessment checklist, instead of relying on ready-made material: Most large organisations would have had Information Security practices for years and practitioners should find a vast amount of existing internal material in that space:

- If the existing internal material is too large or too complex, simplify it

- If it's too vague, enrich it with the right amount of (relevant) good practice

But in all cases, traceability to pre-existing internal material must be regarded as paramount.

It should give stakeholders a sense of continuity and coherence, and value their past efforts where relevant: Ignoring valued pieces of existing documentation that might have taken vast efforts to assemble or replacing them with arbitrary external good practices can only alienate stakeholders.

But practitioners must also assess upfront the pre-existing governance model surrounding all internal material collected: How was it assembled? by whom? when? when was it last updated? what are the internal validation processes surrounding it? how was it communicated to relevant stakeholders?

They must tailor their assessment checklist to focus on the sponsor's objectives and the purpose of the exercise (e.g. Compliance vs. Risk vs. Maturity Assessment, as highlighted above) while respecting:

The validity and relevance of pre-existing material (ensuring such material remains traceable throughout)

The prescribed timeframes and your own resources (both might be constrained by the budget available to perform the exercise)

Simplicity, industry relevance and clarity of language must rule throughout.

This type of exercise will bring the assessment practitioners in contact with the key cyber security players (typically the CISO – or equivalent – and their team), and will give them an important vehicle to win their trust by showing they understand their capabilities and constraints. This degree of trust (between the assessor and the assessed) will be fundamental to the accuracy and honesty of the assessment itself. From the accuracy of the assessment will be derived the results relevance and actionability, and from there the genuine value of the exercise to the business as a whole.

5. The practice of the assessment itself: Listen, Listen, Listen

Cyber security is a complex topic, where problems are often rooted in decades of short-termism, under-investment, adverse prioritization, or excessive focus on arbitrary technical solutions at the expense of sound governance practices and common sense.

In any large organisation, the assessment practitioners are likely to come across a complex historical context, and often a vast amount of technical and personal legacy. It is essential to capture – or at least understand – the "softer" (human) aspects:

Practitioners should analyse their checklist and group subjects by themes.

They should identify relevant stakeholders, book meetings in advance and meet with them on their turf, preferably face to face to form a personal bond even if it forces them to travel.

They must not follow the structure of their checklist to the letter: Instead, they should ask open questions, let the stakeholders talk, and LISTEN, LISTEN, LISTEN before re-assembling the stakeholders' input to match the intended output of the checklist.

Practitioners are also likely to find situations where a number of initiatives or projects are already underway in the cyber security space. They must understand their scope, their context, their degree of advancement, and the stakeholders involved.

They should record fairly without burying bad news and give due credit to unstructured practices where they are efficient.

Overall, the assessment team must be kept small and compact even for large scale assessments; meeting notes should be recorded ASAP and shared with other members of the assessment team.

Validation must take place transparently with key stakeholders throughout the assessment and step by step: It will ensure they buy into the overall approach, drive a common interpretation of the assessment checklist and ultimately engineer a stronger acceptance of the findings.

6. Analysing and presenting results: Do not catch senior management unaware

The assessment practitioners must understand upfront what works best in terms of presentation format for the organisation being assessed, i.e. the type of format that is already being used, that senior management would recognise and be comfortable with.

Assessment results must be formally linked to the threats identified upfront, and work underway – initiatives and projects; good or bad – must be acknowledged.

The strength of graphical models should be used to allow "what-if" scenarios to be visualised, typically around quick wins (should there be any) or projects already underway.

Again, simplicity and clarity of language must rule throughout. The focus must be on hard facts and the hard reality of the assessment results, instead of fuzzy numbers, arbitrary "ROI" calculations and other highly disputable business justifications.

Fundamental to results acceptance is not to catch senior management unaware if results are bad: Nobody likes to be "embarrassed" publicly in meetings; instead senior assessment team leaders should book briefing sessions ahead of key validation meetings with relevant stakeholders and allow them to voice their views in private.

7. Creating change dynamics and driving real action

Real and lasting change in the cyber security space can be complex and take time to be delivered: It is fundamental to put actions in the right perspective in terms of timeframes and build on work underway – good or bad – as much as realistically possible.

The focus must not be purely on technical solutions: Technology should support and enable sound security processes. Large organisations facing complex cross-silos problems (e.g. in the Identity & Access Management space) must resist the urge to build security processes around technical platforms for the sake of winning time: This is rarely the case, and many large companies have been getting it wrong for the last 15 years (and in many instances pushed by shameless vendors).

Equally, the focus must not be on looking for arbitrary quick wins, as there may not be any.

Instead, the focus must be on looking into the past for roadblocks that have prevented progress and finding ways to remove them or circumnavigate them, challenging the organisational status-quo if necessary: People and organisational structures in place may be unable to lead change and it could be that changing those is the right place to start.

Most cyber security problems will be rooted in culture, governance and process: This is where corrective action should be rooted too to be successful.

Building a support coalition amongst business leaders is fundamental to ensure funding over the mid- to long-term. The approach highlighted above – clear governance established upfront with all stakeholders and constructive assessment leading to genuine findings acceptance – should lead to it naturally.

#54 Managing Risk or managing risks?

2 February 2017

The keys to a successful second line of defence

There are many risk management methodologies in existence but it is not uncommon to come across large firms still following today simplistic, dysfunctional or flawed practices, in particular around operational risk management.

The main issue with many of those approaches is that they are plagued by a fundamental theoretical issue, which goes far beyond semantics: There is an abyss between managing "Risk" (broadly defined as "the impact of uncertainty on objectives") and managing "risks" (events or scenarios that might have an undesirable outcome).

But many practitioners, when faced with the challenges of establishing a second line of defence type-of-function, still follow the path of least resistance and start with the arbitrary definition upfront of a series of "risks", that are generally collected through workshops with senior executives in the business. In practice, that's where many aspects start to go wrong, driven by a short-termist business agenda or a complacent "tick-in-the-box" management culture around compliance.

The dynamics of those workshops often revolve around "what keeps you awake at night" type of discussions, which force the participants to imagine situations where something could go seriously wrong and hit the firm. Participants generally engage with the process based on their own experience and ability to project themselves. Almost always, they draw on past experiences, things they have seen at other companies (in other jobs) or things they have heard of. Rarely are those stories based on hard facts directly pertinent to the firm and its problems. It often results in organic and very rich exchanges but also leads to an avalanche of scenarios, unstructured and often overlapping. The lack of rigour in the approach also results in most cases in a considerable language mix-up, with the description of the so-called "risks" combining shamelessly threats, controls and other elements – internal or external.

Then follows a second phase during which participants are asked to estimate how likely are those scenarios to affect the firm and what could be the resulting financial loss.

The first part ("how likely are those scenarios to affect the firm") is plagued by a fundamental confusion between frequency and probability (in many cases, this is entirely by design i.e. participants being asked "could this happen weekly, monthly, annually?"). Again, participants tend to engage with the question by drawing on past experiences (the "bias of imaginability" theorised by Kahneman) or things they have seen elsewhere, irrespective of the actual context of the firm itself. At best, it results in "educated guesses"; at worst, we end up in pure "finger-in-the-air" territory.

The assessment of the potential financial losses is often more reliable, as this is an area where most of the senior executives involved would have more experience, and as long as the monetary brackets are wide enough, they are likely to put the various scenarios in the right buckets.

At the back of that, a risk "heat map" is drawn, a number of action plans are defined and a budgetary figure is put on each (in terms of the investment required to have an impact of the risk map). This is the point where risk is either "accepted", "mitigated" or in theory "transferred".

In practice, the impact of the proposed scenarios on the risk map is often estimated and rarely quantifiable, and the whole process is simply used to drive or justify a positive or negative investment decision, or to present an illusion of science to auditors or regulators.

The agreed actions are then given to a project manager or to a programme office to supervise, often with some form of progress reporting put in place back to a risk committee, with all sorts of convoluted KPIs and KRIs wrapped around it.

This whole approach is certainly better than doing nothing, but it is flawed at a number of levels. Essentially, it is vulnerable to political window-dressing from start to end, and the various estimations made by senior executives along the chain (willingly or unwillingly) can be used to adjust to any internal political agenda (e.g. presenting a particular picture to regulators, limiting expenditure, not having to confront boards or business units with an inconvenient truth).

Fundamentally, the "risks" being (allegedly) "managed" may have nothing to do with the actual reality of the firm, and even the "management" aspects may be disputable, in particular if the governance around the actual delivery of the agreed action plan is weak or inefficient (or, at the other end of the scale, bureaucratic and overly complex). This is more about "doing stuff" (at best) than "managing Risk" because of the colossal amount of assumptions made along the way.

There are 3 aspects that need to be addressed for those methods to work better and deliver proper results in terms of real "Risk Management":

1. Talking to senior executives and running workshops with them is a good start, but they should be focused on "threats" – and not "risks" – and on the "assets" the "threats" may target. Focusing on threats and assets brings advantages at 2 levels: First it roots the language of the discussion in the reality of what is at stake, instead of hypothetical scenarios. Second, by following simple threat modelling practices, it offers a structure to guide the discussion with some rigour:

   • Who are the people or organisations who could cause you harm? (the threat agents)

   • What are their motivations? Their level of sophistication? The attack vectors they use? The attack surfaces they look for?

   • What could they do to you?

   By combining and ranking those factors, you arrive to a number of key scenarios that are rooted in the reality of the firm and its context, and in the process, you have forced the executives involved to face the reality of the firm, the world it operates in, and its real viciousness.

   But for the result to be truly representative and meaningful, it is also essential to ensure that all stakeholders are involved across all geographies and corporate silos (business units, IT, Legal, HR, procurement, etc…), and to include key external business partners where business processes or IT facilities have been outsourced.

Asking executive management to place the resulting scenarios in broad financial loss buckets is a good step that is likely to work well as we indicated before, and could be kept, but the assessment of any form of probability of occurrence or potential impact should be dissociated from the discussion with executives at this stage and, again, firmly rooted in the reality of the firm through an independent assessment of the actual presence or absence of the necessary protective measures.

This is essential in focusing management on the fact that "managing Risk" is about protecting the firm from undesirable outcomes, and that it is achieved through the actual implementation of tangible measures that are known to protect, and can be:

- determined upfront based on the identified threat scenarios,

- mandated by policy or adherence to good practice,

- enforced through good governance, internally and with third-parties.

Risk is a by-product of the presence or absence of such measures, and the actual Risk "heat map" for the firm can be drawn in a quantified manner from those independent assessments, instead of being estimated.

2. Once the Risk "heat map" is firmly linked to the presence or absence of actual protective measures, it is possible to define risk treatment scenarios also linked to those measures and map in a quantified manner the impact they would have on the Risk "heat map".

Fig. 10: The Risk Management Cycle

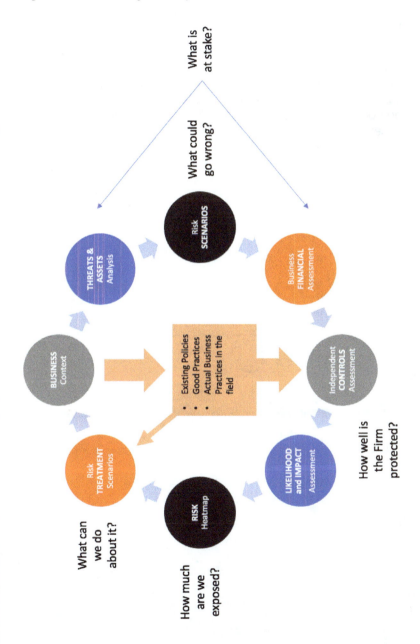

It is then possible to compare those Risk treatment scenarios and determine the most attractive for the firm. It also becomes possible to track and visualise progress in a quantifiable manner.

It is easy to argue that the governance issues around the actual delivery of agreed Risk treatment actions still remain (in particular for larger firms), and that the two approaches are fundamentally the same (one qualitative, and the other quantitative), but the quantitative approach is truer to its purpose ("managing Risk"), considerably richer in terms of managerial levers, and far less vulnerable to manipulation and window-dressing.

#55 The "Three Lines of Defence" model only works on Trust

20 April 2017

It is no big secret that the "Three Lines of Defence" model underpinning many GRC practices in large firms is poorly understood and poorly applied at grass-root levels.

Anecdotal evidence we observe in the field every day suggests that many organisations operate it in a variety of hybrid fashions – knowingly or unknowingly – and experience a range of dysfunctions that seriously limit the value the model is designed to bring.

These dysfunctions all revolve around the same problem in our experience: A form of defiance between the parties, which builds up over time and is rooted in inconsistencies, lack of clarity around reporting models, language issues, and a lack of over-arching investment coherence at Board level.

For example, it is not uncommon to find situations where 1st line controls are fundamentally weak or missing in some areas. This is something the 2nd line must identify and report on, but at the same time, the 2nd line cannot become prescriptive with regards to the implementation of the relevant 1st line controls (even if the actual nature of the 2nd line controls themselves may always influence the determination of the 1st line controls to be put in place). It is unavoidable, in those situations, that 1st line stakeholders may feel singled-out and exposed, in particular if (for example):

- Those deficiencies are going to be reported in the simplistic format of a RAG report to a body of management where they are not represented

- The topic at hand is genuinely complex, multi-dimensional and rooted in decades of adverse legacy (and may be impossible to explain in simple terms to senior executives coming from a totally different background)

- The same issues were not identified in an earlier targeted audit performed by the 3rd line

Their management is clearly pushing them towards other priorities, sometimes coupled with aggressive cost reductions

It is easy to look at this list and think that most of it revolves around ordinary day-to-day political dysfunctions that are common to many large firms, and impossible to avoid to a large extent. After all, the "Three Lines of Defence" model is not designed to avoid those issues, but to highlight them so that they can be treated (maybe).

But it remains unavoidable that, over time, these dynamics create the conditions for distrust to build up at the interface between the lines of defence, in particular if personalities don't match or where differences in personal backgrounds create language issues or other barriers.

Distrust breeds window-dressing, and in the long-run, could bring data quality or relevance issues that may seriously skew risk reporting and mislead investors or shareholders.

These situations are generally hard to unlock, with 2nd and 3rd line functions often entrenched in dogmatic separation of duties considerations. There are two lines of action to treat the problem:

Heads of Risk, Compliance or Internal Audit should ensure that counterparts across the lines come from a similar background and professional culture: For example, the 2nd or 3rd line staff should have faced the same day-to-day challenges as their 1st line counterparts at some point in their career, and should therefore relate to those more naturally and more practically. Using only life-long auditors or life-long consultants to staff those layers often creates the conditions highlighted above.

Where 1st line maturity is really low towards controls and 1st line stakeholders are genuinely struggling with the concepts involved, Heads of Risk, Compliance or Internal Audit should sponsor the set-up of a separate "Controls Architecture" function (independent from their respective teams) which would assist stakeholders in that respect.

Separation of duties is important, and often looked at dogmatically by regulators; but an overarching principle of efficiency has to prevail, in particular where senior management is genuinely driving a culture of change around controls. In an earlier post, we have highlighted how this principle of efficiency could be applied, for example where the Infosec function is structured within the portfolio of the CIO.

Hybrid models can work and bring value around GRC – more than watertight and dogmatic separated models – but as long as the dynamics of trust and efficiency are preserved.

#56 Cyber Security: How do you build a transformational dynamic?

19 October 2017

Security is not about "enabling" the business but "protecting" it

At the end of a keynote speech I gave at the excellent CIOWaterCooler LIVE! Event in London on 28th September 2017 on security organisation, governance and creating the dynamics for change around cyber security, I was asked a challenging question on which I would like to elaborate:

It is true that it is one thing – complex enough – to lead and deliver the cyber security transformation of an organisation that has reached the point where it knows it needs to change, but it is another one – equally complex – to create the condition for such realisation to take place.

Where the business mindset is rooted in short-termism and senior executives are unable to look beyond quick wins and the figures for the next month or the next quarter, how do you get them to the point where they realise that without a greater emphasis on security controls, their business will eventually fall victim to cyber criminals, that cyber-attacks are fast becoming a simple matter of WHEN (not IF), and that the associated impact – financial, reputational – is increasingly impossible to quantify ?

I don't think this is a battle that can be won through a rational engagement and that essentially, it is rooted in breaking down deep cognitive biases; a situation that has been well analysed by Nobel prize laureate Daniel Kahneman amongst others.

In a pure bottom-up approach, it is my opinion that many CIOs or CISOs are simply wasting their time trying to articulate how security could be a "business-enabler" or trying to calculate some hypothetical "ROI" on security investments. More often than not, these exercises only add a vernacular of business language over the same old tech storyline, and when it comes to ROI calculations, those are often open to considerable margins of errors or plagued by untested and unverified modelling techniques.

This is not the way, in my opinion, you break those cognitive biases and the problem needs to be approached over time in a completely different manner.

Where security maturity is low but the business is incapable or unwilling to prioritise in favour of much needed long-term security transformation efforts, the key is for the CISO and the CIO is to act at two levels:

First, they must keep their head down, and on a daily basis, continue to deliver on those tactical projects the business want them to drive. They must be successful at that. They must develop a positive and successful relationship with their business. They must be seen as adding value (whatever value means to the stakeholders).

At the same time and in parallel to those delivery efforts, they must constantly focus their language towards the business on the reality of the threats it may be facing.

Not on risk which ultimately for the business will always be something that may or may not happen, something you can transfer, mitigate, insure against; not necessarily something you need to DO something about.

And they should stay well clear of cliché-esque business jargon ("security as a business-enabler!") or business concepts they don't master properly ("ROI of security!").

They should stick to their core competences (that's where they will be successful) and always bring the discussion back to the field of reality: After all, cyber threats are real, virulent, targeting almost all business sectors: Cyber security doesn't have to excuse itself for existing!!!

Data breach after data breach, incident after incident, newspaper article after newspaper article, the CISO and the CIO need to push those real-life events towards business leaders, picking the right battles and the right timing with each executive.

It will require time, political acumen and a true sense of subtle communication with each business leader, but over time, it will chip away at the defences and create the sense with business leaders that threats are real and internal controls insufficient to ensure adequate protection.

Protecting what you care about is a natural thing for most people, and it should gradually shift priorities towards security matters, where before they were structurally stacked against those objectives, even in the most complex business situations.

But the CISO and the CIO must also build their own credibility up throughout the exercise, as it is their trustworthiness and their ability to deliver the must-needed change effort that will be tested.

And that comes through a demonstrable ability to navigate the political complexity of the firm.

A complex task indeed, in particular in large organisations. Not one that needs vague business jargon, but strong and determined leadership.

#57 The Shifting Debate around Security Metrics

7 June 2018

Driving security transformation is becoming key; not justifying investments

The age-long debate around security metrics and dashboards seems very much alive within the CISO community. But it is often positioned in an outdated historical perspective.

For many CISOs, it seems to be still about "justifying investments" or articulating some form of "return on security investment".

For CIOs and many other C-level executives, those ships sailed long ago. The large scale cyberattacks and data breaches of the past decade, coupled with the change in privacy regulation they triggered, have put cyber risk on the Board's agenda and the "When, Not If" paradigm resonates with many board members.

On security matters, "Tell me how much we need to spend" or "Are we spending enough" have become more common questions around the boardroom than "Why do you want to spend so much"…

So why are we still hearing some form of disconnect between the CISO and their bosses on the topic?

Trust is at the heart of the problem here, and the nature of the relationship between the CISO and their boss.

Many CIOs don't have any problem justifying security investments in the face of non-stop cyberattacks. But they know as well that it is getting things done that will protect the firm, not just committing budgetary resources, so the CIO asking the CISO "show me what return we will get for such investment" is sometimes a way of saying something else:

- I don't understand why you want to do this
- I am not sure this is the right thing to do
- I don't think you will deliver it on any meaningful scale

It is often a challenge that is born out of some form of distrust. In our experience, where there is complete and total commonality of views between the CISO and their boss around what needs to be done on security, and full trust around the execution of a common security roadmap, those issues don't arise and the question of "return on security investments" is never asked.

The debate around security metrics – like the whole approach to building and managing a successful security practice – needs to shift from a short-termist project-driven approach, to a long-termist roadmap-driven one.

In such context, you mainly need metrics upstream, to build and sell the long-term security roadmap: Those have to be rooted in the reality of the challenges the firm is facing and backed against a sound appreciation of the threats it faces.

Security measures – and the associated investments they require – will protect the firm from real and active threats. Their implementation will modify the cyber risk, or cyber maturity, or cyber compliance posture of the organisation (depending on what the main drivers are at executive level). That's what the associated metrics need to capture and show.

They can be assessment-based metrics but need to be linkable to actual actions, and the methodology must reflect where necessary – in particular in relation to third-parties – the lack of availability or reliability of assessment data.

Visualisation is also a key factor: It is essential to put actions in the right long-term perspective, and to give management the sense that there is a real purpose behind security measures. This should be accompanied as well by the right governance and operating model, to give management assurance around the actual execution of the proposed roadmap.

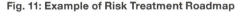

Fig. 11: Example of Risk Treatment Roadmap

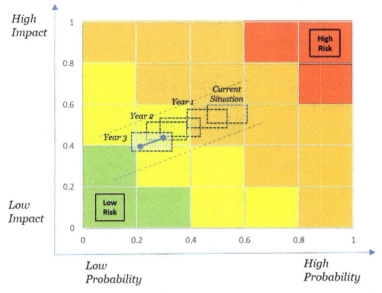

In the example above, the size of each rectangle reflects the uncertainty around data availability or quality, and the evolution of the score for each year would have been associated to actual measures e.g. Year 1 = implementation of an Identity and Access Management model, Year 2 = implementation of a vendor risk management model, etc...

You will also need metrics downstream, to show actual progress against the roadmap but those should be standard programme management metrics, and many large organisations will have well established methodologies in place in support of that.

Overall, selling success will be key, and going back to the original scoring model used to build and sell the roadmap, will give senior executives a sense of continuity and management solidity.

Way beyond the justification of ad-hoc investments and pet-projects for the CISO, metrics have to be at the heart of the sound security practice, but they must be focused on tracking progress in time in support of a long-term transformative vision.

#58 What to look out for when hiring a new CISO?

21 June 2018

The traditional role of the CISO is changing.

It is being challenged by emerging new regulations such as GDPR, which are impacting all industry sectors, and the arrival on the scene of the new role of the DPO in many firms.

It is being marginalised by long-term digital transformation trends which are changing the historical role of the CIO, and the emergence of broader corporate concepts, such as resilience, which are bringing out a more holistic way to address business protection matters from the Board down.

At the same time, the CISO role has never been more important, in the wake of non-stop cyberattacks and data breaches.

Hiring a new CISO could be hard for many firms and finding the right person will involve a careful approach, articulated around the following principles.

The broad profile of the role must be clear: Fire fighter, figurehead or change agent?

First of all, the hiring manager must be clear about the nature and objectives of the role, and the context in which the hire is taking place. It could be that the firm has never had a CISO before. It could be that a new role is being created, for example at Group level. It could be that the departing CISO was perceived as highly successful and that their departure is a big loss. It could be that the departing CISO had been in the job for many years but had achieved very little in practice.

At high level, the hiring manager must define the broad profile of the role: Fire fighter? Figure head? Change agent?

In all cases, security is becoming a far more complex and transversal matter and getting results will mean that the CISO will have to work across corporate silos, with IT, HR, other support functions, business units and geographies. The managerial complexity of the role and the level of experience required to be successful must be acknowledged.

Management experience is paramount; more than raw technical knowledge

The role of the CISO is no longer some form of low-grade tech job. Even more, it is no longer a role for a junior executive, a life-long consultant or an ex-auditor: It will require grit and a true field experience to achieve anything. And preferably a good amount of knowledge of the industry sector and corporate politics. Those only come with real-life management experience.

Judging by what we see in the field, an internal assignment is generally more productive, and less risky, as the new CISO will know the firm and will be known to key stakeholders. But it means the CISO role must have a truly senior profile to attract the best internally, that incentives package and role visibility have to be right, and that the reporting line must match all those factors.

The new CISO does not have to be a technologist or someone already in a CISO role. As a matter of fact, key will be in their ability to articulate the business value of security, and that should come more naturally to business leaders. Control-mindedness, personal gravitas and political acumen are likely to be important success attributes for the CISO, probably as important – if not more – than their raw technical knowledge of the security field.

Think outside the box and take your time

This is definitely the type of search for which thinking outside the box could be rewarded, and where most will come – in terms of long-term success – from the personal profile of the individual involved.

Overall, take your time. It is likely the role will be difficult to fill and rushing into appointing someone "because you need to" will only lead to mistakes. Use an interim CISO if necessary until the right person is found, but you must not hire in a hurry.

This is all the more important for organisations which have never had a CISO before, or those which have been stuck in a decade long spiral of failure around security matters.

It is also essential for those creating a new CISO role for example at Group level, or those moving towards a CSO type of organisational model, as highlighted here by McKinsey and Co.

The CISO role has never been more important.

The firms that fail at appointing a new CISO are those which rush and push an inexperienced techie in a poorly defined role.

Positioning the role accurately in relation to the firm's objectives around security, thinking it as a senior leadership role, and taking the time to find the right leader are the keys to long-term success.

#59 The 4 Pillars of a Lasting Cyber Security Transformation

8 November 2018

Simply throwing money at the problem is rarely the answer

Many CIOs and CISOs would have come across this situation after an incident, a serious near-miss or a bad audit report: Suddenly, money and resources – which were previously scarce – appear out of nowhere, priorities shift, and senior executives demand urgent action around cyber security.

It is probably the dream of many CISOs to inherit one day such transformational challenge where money is – apparently – no object. In practice, however, it can also be a curse if you fail to deliver.

What are the key factors in driving successful transformation around cyber security?

Setting the right timeframes

First, the CISO must assess without complacency the true nature of the transformation required, the depth of commitment of senior management, and the timeframes which would be required to deliver real and lasting change – independently of stakeholders expectations.

This is the first area where the CISO will need to manage expectations with senior executives. Change takes "the time it takes", in particular where culture and behaviours are involved, and some aspects associated with cyber security transformation could be complex, disturb existing business practices and lead to substantial projects (for example around Identity and Access Management or Data Leak Prevention).

In our experience, the complete top-down re-engineering of an entire security practice can take up to 3 to 5 years in any large organisation. Nobody can be expected to achieve anything significant in 6 months to a year if initial maturity levels are very low; 2 years may not be enough either.

The first management challenge of the CISO is to get senior stakeholders to understand that fact. This is about a real commitment to change at least as much as it is about resources, and the ability to think strategically over the mid- to long-term. Not all senior executives or board members are capable of doing that. The CISO will have to find the right allies and use their influence to get the message across.

Merely "fixing" illusory quick-wins never amounts to lasting transformation.

The realisation of the timeframes involved will be rooted in the appreciation by senior management of the tasks involved, and such appreciation needs to be backed against a sound and meaningful assessment of the starting point.

From there, a transformative vision and roadmap can be drawn looking towards the right horizon.

Focusing on clear transformative themes and explicit goals

In situations where the organisation needs to face fundamental change around cyber security, it will be essential to set clear and simple objectives to all parties.

Trying to fix everything at the same time, irrespective of interdependencies and the inherent complexity of some issues, and possibly over unrealistic timeframes, will simply lead to confusion and failure.

Instead, the CISO should start by assessing dependencies between the various parts of the transformative roadmap and group action around broad themes which in turn will focus priorities and investments.

Those themes should be clear, simple to articulate, and structured around explicit goals and milestones.

Delivering through an empowered senior team

Although there will be projects involved in delivering the transformative roadmap, the ultimate objective is to create a sustainable, self-standing transformed security practice. To this end, the re-engineering of their team needs to be the first task for the CISO so that transformation can be delivered through the reshaped team and not only through contingent project resources and consultants.

Defining the right team structure, operating and governance model should be top-priority for the CISO, involving all relevant stakeholders across IT, business and support functions, and also involving all relevant geographies and third-parties.

Staffing the new team should follow and start top-down, so that the CISO can delegate the transformative burden to empowered senior direct reports. This layer of management once established will take on the duties to staff the rest of their teams and to deliver explicit parts of the transformative roadmap. Finding those people – internally or externally – in the current recruitment market could be tough and take time, so starting as early as possible on this phase should be key for the CISO.

From there, the delivery of the transformative roadmap can start, but it will be equally crucial for the CISO to ensure that all key personnel are incentivised to stay the course, as there might be rough waters ahead.

Sticking to the plan

Establishing realistic timeframes, setting clear goals and finding the right people to drive the transformative efforts through a structured team are key. In parallel, the CISO should continue to get all parties on board behind the right transformative roadmap. This phase could easily take up to 6 months, but it is essential to long-term success.

There may be quick-wins, or there may not be. The CISO must resist inventing some where there are none and must also avoid knee-jerk reactions which may only damage the long-term case.

One thing this is NOT about is implementing more tech; at least not upfront.

There is no magical technology platform or service provider which can be – on its own – the answer to a fundamental transformative challenge around cyber security.

Technology will – of course – have a role to play in the transformative effort in most organisations, but the CISO and their team must come to that in due course, and in the right context, set in the right transformative vision, roadmap and operating model. Jumping at tech solutions and tech vendors upfront cannot be the first thing to do.

The overarching challenge for the CISO behind all this lies in getting senior management to see that long-term change is rooted in a long-term vision and long-term planning which takes time to establish.

It may be a hard sell in absence of tactical quick-wins, and a lot will rest on the trust between the CISO and their boss, as well as the personal profile, managerial experience and political acumen of the CISO.

Given the complexities involved, which are not just technical, but also often rooted in culture and governance, delivering lasting change will always require a structured approach and relentless drive to succeed.

Simply throwing money at the problem in the hope of making it disappear, without a proper consideration of those matters simply leads to failure and can only aggravate the perception by senior stakeholders that security is just a cost and a burden.

#60 The Business Value of Cybersecurity

22 November 2018 [with Vincent Viers]

Tangible business metrics are key but hard to find

Cybersecurity is rising as a key issue on the radar of virtually all organisations. According to a recent AT Kearney report, cyber-attacks have been topping executives' lists of business risks for three straight years. This concern is also driven by security and privacy becoming increasingly valued by customers, and by regulators stepping into the topic (GDPR in Europe, California Consumer Privacy Act of 2018).

Beyond this, it is now becoming crystal clear that cybersecurity – beyond good practice and good ethics – is quite simply good business. As a recent Cisco study made clear, cybersecurity will help fuel (and protect) an estimated $5.3trillion in private sector digital Value at Stake in the next 10 years. This is the kind of numbers boards cannot afford to overlook.

Tangible estimates like this one, however, are painfully rare in the cyber security space. Indeed, concepts relating to cybersecurity are both multi-facetted and very elusive – making them notoriously hard to measure. Furthermore, good cybersecurity is defined by the absence of breaches or losses. Observing what is not happening is a challenging – if interesting – endeavour.

A stringent example of this measurement problem can be found in a recent BCG research on *Total Societal Impact*. To their credit, cybersecurity is mentioned fairly extensively throughout the report as a key component of a firms' ESG (Environmental, Social & Governance) strategy – although not consistently across industry sectors.

The issue arises when it comes to quantifying that intuition. The BCG for example reports finding a significant link between "Securing business and personal data" and a firm's valuation. Looking into the appendix of the report, the problem lies in the fact that this concept seems to be operationalized through a series of somewhat vague dummy (0/1) variables. Examples of such metrics include *whether* "measures to ensure customer security" have been taken, or *whether* an information security management system has been implemented.

This is not only overly-simplistic – hiding key nuances in levels of cybersecurity maturity across firms – but it also encourages "tick-in-the-box" approaches to cybersecurity which have plagued the field for ages. Tellingly, no quantitative results are actually presented for cybersecurity in the report.

This lack of details around the quantification of the tangible value of following cybersecurity best practices is a problem. In fact, we believe it is an important reason why the issue is still shifting in and out of most boards' radars. Gut feeling alone does not make for a strong-enough case: Top executives are increasingly asking "*Show me the data*".

Beyond the fact that measuring success in the cybersecurity is very hard, another issue is the stringent lack of meaningful data.

This is a really big problem in the field of cyber insurance, for example, which struggles to fit its traditional actuarial models around the scarce data they can get a hold of. The reason for that is quite simple: most organizations are still very reluctant to share what they perceive as highly sensitive cybersecurity data (assuming they even have them to start with).

We also talked about this problem in the context of training defensive AI for cybersecurity, but this scarcity of reliable InfoSec data hinders generally much-needed research and results.

Being able to show key stakeholders in business terms what exactly is the tangible value-added of cybersecurity will be key in finally anchoring the topic at the right level of organizations.

Money – *and data* – talk. And boards usually listen. But we're not there yet and cybersecurity looks definitely like a promising path for data-driven research.

#61 The Two Factors Killing GRC Practices

31 January 2019

Excessive complexity and lack of first line integration render many GRC metrics useless

Many CISOs complain of communication problems with their business. They are not being listened to. They are not getting the budget they think they should get. They feel their business prioritises against security too often.

It has been a recurring theme amongst information security professionals for the best part of the last 15 years, and it is rooted in a wide range of factors, amongst which the profile of the CISO is often a dominant limitation.

Many CISOs are simply too technical: They know they need to bridge the gap with their business, but they often return to their comfort zone at the first opportunity: For them, "threats" is often translated into malware, phishing and hackers, while the business wants to hear insider fraud or intellectual property theft.

This often leads to the CISO role being ringfenced and limited to its first line technical remit, while GRC functions develop in second line of defence.

But those functions themselves very often struggle to develop meaningful conversations with their business around cyber security.

GRC teams tend to have an ivory-towered view of the problem and to rely on ready-made overly complex methodologies, loosely related to the reality of first line activities.

They rush into buying some tech platform which is supposed to "enable" the GRC process, but in reality, the jargon of those products and methodologies is often meaningless to the business. Impact assessments and risk assessments can be inextricably complex. The quality of the data collected is often questionable as a result, and many of those approaches never scale up for good in large firms due to the sheer human cost of deploying them.

The lack of hard-wiring to first line activities make the GRC metrics produced artificial, and unusable in practice to recommend, justify or manage first line investment. If, in addition, the scope covered is limited due to deployment or acceptance issues, the overall value of such metrics can be highly disputable – beyond the proverbial "tick-in-the-box" which they will invariably provide.

None of that helps the business understand and manage their cyber risk posture. Over time, distrust sets in and, as the "when-not-if" paradigm around cyber-attacks takes root in the boardroom, senior executives need to find a way out.

It can only involve refocusing GRC practices towards simplicity so they can be effectively and efficiently deployed on a large scale across the real breadth of the firm – and possibly towards its supply chain.

It will also involve refocusing GRC practices towards a proper and meaningful integration with first line cyber security data, so that GRC metrics reflect the reality of the first line of defence.

The "when-not-if" paradigm makes the Board increasingly willing to invest to ensure the protection of the firm from cyber threats, but it also shifts priorities towards measuring progress and ensuring things get done.

In many firms, the equation between Governance, Risk and Compliance around cyber security is becoming heavily weighted towards the G, and GRC functions must adjust as a result, both in terms of internal structures and in terms of interactions with other stakeholders.

In particular, first line and second line must work together on this. They must trust each other and look beyond absurd and arbitrary "separation of duties" concepts, to produce meaningful data for the business, around which meaningful decisions will be made to protect the firm.

#62 The Hard Truth Around Cyber Security Awareness Programmes

10 October 2019

5 key points to drive culture change around cyber security

Culture and governance are key to drive change around cyber security behaviours, but too many awareness programmes focus simply on superficial technical gimmicks. Let's start by deconstructing 3 clichés which have been dominating the security awareness arena for the past decade.

Cliché #1 – Cyber Security is Everybody's Responsibility

At face value, this is truly a very dangerous argument to manipulate. To answer it using another cliché, there is a fine line between something being everybody's responsibility, and the same thing becoming nobody's responsibility.

The key here is to acknowledge that while each employee may have a role to play in securing the firm's assets, those roles do vary from function to function, and failure to communicate with each staff member in meaningful ways in the context of their own job will simply not work: Telling HR staff who receive CVs by email everyday not to open attachments is a waste of time.

Also, it is essential to acknowledge that the level of engagement of each employee around cyber security will depend entirely on the level of engagement the employee has with the firm, its culture and its values. It is a natural instinct to protect what you care about. Conversely, it can be a hard job to convince disengaged staff, or staff who see senior management constantly allowed to skip the rules, while they have to adhere to stricter measures.

So it may well be that in some form "Cyber Security is Everyone's Responsibility", but the message cannot be generic and has to be structured appropriately. In addition, the example has to come from the top and must be relayed without exception by all middle-management layers for the message of good practice to work through the fabric of the firm.

That's often the most common flaw of many cyber security awareness campaigns: They are owned by the cyber security team and structured horizontally towards all staff, instead of being owned by a board member and structured to cascade vertically through line management. Ownership for Cyber Security has to start at the top. Period. One board member should be visibly in charge, and part of their compensation package should ride on it, as we advocated in an earlier article.

HR management should be involved as well, and they have a key role to play: Specific key responsibilities and accountabilities around cyber security should be distributed across staff members and articulated formally in role descriptions. Staff should be incentivised through compensation and by middle-management to address those aspects of their roles as an integral part of their job, not as a piece of meaningless management jargon.

Readers may think this is just idealistic and cannot work in most firms, because those layers of management simply would not be interested or would not understand cyber security sufficiently to articulate a meaningful vision around it.

They may well be right in many cases, but it is also the role of the CISO to stimulate, structure and support that type of engagement.

Of course, firms looking to engage in that type of top-down approach to cyber security awareness development will need to have the right CISO in terms of personal profile, personal gravitas and management experience, or may need to evolve their security organisation to bring in a broader CSO role.

Those necessary exchanges between the security leadership team and senior management will constitute a fundamental awareness programme just by themselves, but any security awareness development campaign can only be truly successful with a visible and credible board member as a figurehead.

If senior management – including HR management – or middle-management are not prepared to engage in a meaningful manner with the fundamental aspects of security good practice, any message anybody may try to drive towards the staff could simply prove to be an expensive waste of money.

Cliché #2 – People are the Weakest Link

They may well be, but the key is to understand why and how in the context of each firm, before jumping to ready-made solutions, in particular with tech vendors.

It has to start from a sound examination of the threats each business is facing. The insider threat may well be a widespread high-ranking business threat in financial services, not so much maybe in logistics or retail.

Of course, in all firms there will be people who have access to sensitive business information and may be tempted or coerced in certain circumstances to leak it out. But the key here is to understand and address their potential motivations in doing so.

Those motivations – quite often – will be rooted in corporate culture, management styles and governance problems. As many areas you are not likely to address through a "traditional" tech-focused cyber security awareness programme...

It is worth repeating this one more time: Staff will protect the firm with a natural instinct, if they care about it and share its values and its purpose – economically, and increasingly socially as well.

If that sense of care is not there, if the corporate or management culture is toxic, if employees don't have a sense that they know where the business is going, either because it is not well managed, or because its industry sector at large is not doing well, a broader communication initiative addressing staff disengagement is required and specialised or siloed awareness programmes focusing simply on cyber security are not likely to succeed.

The key will be to bring staff onboard with a valid corporate purpose they can understand and endorse. The need to protect the firm in general as well as its information assets could be one aspect but immersed into a broader campaign aimed at developing a real sense of belonging with employees.

Here again, HR, corporate communications and senior management at large have a key role to play. One senior executive must visibly own and drive the initiative. Once again, this cannot be siloed and left to the CISO and their team.

Cliché #3 – This is all about "Awareness"

How can it be that some firms – and their CISOs – still believe that their staff – apparently – do not KNOW what to do to protect their organisation from cyber threats?

Many people – at individual level – have experienced fraud attempts or virus attacks; data breaches and cyber-attacks are constantly in the news, and many online platforms and service providers have strengthened considerably various of their security measures, for example around multi-factor authentication; increasingly, people are getting used to those additional layers of security in their everyday life.

More importantly, security good practices have been well established for 2 decades and have not evolved that much: "Don't write down your password" meant the same 10 or 20 years ago...

And large firms have spent collectively hundreds of millions across the last 2 decades on so called "security awareness" programmes, not to mention governments and their agencies.

So where did it go wrong with those programmes?

The problem is that most of those – over time – have focused too much on making sure people simply KNOW what to do around security, and not so much in giving them incentives to ACT on it, or dealing with the roadblocks preventing staff from enacting good practice.

Just "knowing" what to do to protect your organisation is simply not enough; only the right actions and behaviours can protect the business, so "awareness" by itself is never going to be sufficient without incentives to act and – where necessary – culture change.

In addition, as detailed above, many of those programmes have often fallen short of expectations by being too generic and not rooted in the right cultural context.

Fake phishing campaigns are a good example of where it goes wrong: They have been all the rage for the past few years but often they contribute to the build-up of a "nasty" culture around cyber security: Employees feel tricked and embarrassed, and those are not emotions which are likely to build a favourable ground in which to root good security practices.

Sending random emails, forcing people to follow online training programmes, putting up posters or distributing mouse-mats may well put ticks in compliance boxes but what does that achieve in real life?

Success criteria ("What-Good-Looks-Like") remain vague, qualitative or anecdotal in many campaigns (for those that are not designed as a pure box-checking exercise to address some cheap audit point)

That shouldn't be the case, and as a matter of fact, the issue of metrics should be central to any cyber security awareness programme and built in from the start.

But it is a really difficult topic, which is why it is frequently side-stepped.

The only way to address this is a meaningful manner – for firms large enough to do this – is to fall back on traditional marketing and polling methods:

- Build representative panels of employees across the firm

- Measure their level of "security awareness" through questionnaires and interviews, in a structured way prior to launching the campaign

- Design the campaign to be centred on key findings highlighted by panels and interviews, and deploy it

- Measure levels of security awareness again and compare

Of course, as well as difficult, this may be expensive, and priced-in from the start, it may well push any programme out of an acceptable budgetary bracket.

But cutting out the metrics aspects – on grounds of costs – from a cyber security awareness programme should bring out a real management question to address: Is it worth spending large amounts on an initiative of that nature, knowing and accepting from the start that you won't be able to measure its success quantitatively?

5 key points to build a successful cyber security culture change programme

In summary:

- A board member must visibly own the campaign and act as a figurehead, with the involvement of HR, corporate communications and the cyber security team: It can only work top-down. Accountabilities and responsibilities around cyber security must be clear.

- Stay clear of empirical and ready-made solutions: Start with focus groups, questionnaires and interviews and measure upfront levels of staff security maturity and engagement with corporate values.

- Centre your campaign on the findings of the initial survey and define success metrics from the start based on measured maturity levels: Your scope may need to be much broader than just cyber security to deliver on staff engagement if initial levels are low.

- Make the messages specific, achievable and rooted in the real life of each team, driven by line management, NOT the CISO and their team

- Build incentives for staff to ACT: It cannot be just about TELLING people what to do

#63 In Defence of Maturity-based Approaches for Cyber Security

24 October 2019

It doesn't make sense to oppose maturity & risk-based approaches to cyber security

This interesting piece from McKinsey made me think and deserves some comments: "The risk-based approach to cybersecurity[1]" (Jim Boehm, Nick Curcio, Peter Merrath, Lucy Shenton, and Tobias Stähle – October 2019).

The risk-based approach itself which it promotes has solid foundations, and in fact is nothing new. Actually, it echoes in many ways the model we – at Corix Partners – have been developing and delivering with clients and associates for the past 10 years

But I don't think it makes sense – or indeed helps the industry move forward – to oppose maturity-based approaches and risk-based approaches. And the characterization of maturity-based models as "a dog that had its day" is frankly excessive.

The assumption that risk-based approaches are somehow more advanced than maturity-based ones, and represent an "evolution" of cyber security practices is highly disputable, and the quantification of maturity-based approaches as leading to over-engineering and over-spending by a factor 3 compared to risk-based approaches is simply misleading (a foot note actually refers to the costs mentioned as "illustrative and extrapolated from real-world examples and estimates").

As a matter of fact, those two approaches are just different ways of managing, driving and measuring action around cyber security in different situations and different firms. One does not have to be superior to the other.

---

1 https://www.mckinsey.com/business-functions/risk/our-insights/the-risk-based-approach-to-cybersecurity

The keys are elsewhere: The approach one firm decides to follow has to be right in relation to the firm's management and governance culture, and its objectives around cyber security. Those will vary naturally from one organization to another, and from one management team to the next.

One trend we are observing more and more is actually the weakening of traditional risk and compliance drivers around cyber security with senior executives. The "when-not-if" paradigm around cyber-attacks is strongly taking root in many boardrooms, and many firms are committing very large amounts to large-scale transformative security programmes; but in return, the board expects execution and protection, and are holding CIOs and CISOs accountable for both.

In those situations, risk often goes to the background, delivery takes centre-stage, and maturity-based approaches generally work well, as long as they revolve around a clear set of capabilities to be developed through the delivery of clear tangible actions to achieve a clear target maturity level.

This is not an approach which will work well only in situations where initial maturity levels are low: It can continue to work throughout the maturity spectrum up to advanced levels. And as long as the capabilities and the actions required to develop them are backed against the firm's objective around cyber security and the real threats it is facing, there is no reason to assume that it would lead to a greater degree of over-engineering – and over-spending – compared to other approaches.

As a matter of fact, whether a firm takes a maturity-driven route or a risk-driven route to ensure it is well protected from cyber threats, none of that changes the nature, the reality or the virulence of those threats, and as a result, the nature of the measures the firm needs to have in place to be well protected. Those necessary protective measures may end-up ordered or prioritised differently, in order to improve maturity or reduce risk, but barring political manipulation by stakeholders, they will be the same and will cost the same.

The chosen approach simply needs to be right to give the executives in charge the levers they need to understand and manage the firm's cyber security posture.

It is our experience that simplicity, clarity and consistency are often the real factors behind successful approaches, and at that game, maturity-based models often win because they can be action-driven from the start, faster to put in place, and less vulnerable to window-dressing by stakeholders.

#64 Does the role of the "Virtual CISO" make any sense?

28 November 2019

Outsourcing something simply because you don't understand it is rarely a good start.

Faced by constant reports of cyber-attacks in the media, most small and medium-size organisations have woken up to the reality of cyber threats over the past few years.

Many still don't really know what to do to protect themselves and turn to "virtual CISO" services for assistance.

While this is better than doing nothing or relying blindly on the security of cloud providers, those externalised, part-time services – often delivered remotely – are rarely the magic bullet they pretend to be…

And let's eliminate upfront any language ambiguity: The idea of a "virtual" solution to a concrete problem created by real threats is dangerous, and the "virtual CISO" shortcut is definitely one the security industry should try to eliminate: Beyond marketing and hype, either you need a CISO or you don't, but their role – and their actions – cannot be "virtual" to counteract real threats.

Moving on from those considerations, the concept of an externalised, part-time and partly remote CISO role is generally attractive to small and medium-size organisations for numerous reasons:

First, rightly or wrongly, they often see cyber security as a complex technical matter and feel that they do not have the right skills in-house; at the same time, they also think they do not need a full-time security role given their size. Of course, both aspects of that statement are disputable: It is not rare to find IT analysts with cyber security as their hobby who could make perfectly suitable CISOs in small firms; and the scale of the role depends of the level of maturity of each firm, its regulatory obligations and its security ambitions.

Second, an externalised role is seen by many as a cheaper and more flexible, task-driven stepping stone for them to understand what the CISO job really entails and the value it can bring, before committing further.

Finally, for some, externalising the position is also a way of ensuring a degree of independence with regards to internal politics.

Those last two aspects are defendable and may lead to positioning the role at a level where it really adds value. But organisations must also consider the following points to avoid taking a wrong direction:

"We can't afford a full-time role" is an excuse often heard around the appointment of a so-called "virtual CISO"

But this is not just about what one organisation can "afford": Anybody who has spent enough time in the security industry would know that money appears out of nowhere at the first sight of an incident – or of an audit point in some firms…

And how can you determine how much to spend on security until you really understand what you need to do to protect yourself and meet your regulatory obligations?

Outsourcing something simply because you don't understand it is rarely a good start.

The decision around right-sizing and externalising – or not – the role of the CISO must primarily be about what one organisation wants and needs to achieve around cyber security, and the message it wants to send to its ecosystem on that matter.

Having a CISO of some sort will always be better than not having one when it comes to demonstrating adherence to security values but relying on an externalised part-time service could send a weak confidence signal to customers, partners or potential investors.

Then it is worth considering the real nature of the role itself, even in small to medium-size organisations: It cannot be reduced to tasks and projects; "Security by Design" and "Privacy by Design" principles are becoming the norm, and to work well, the role of the CISO must be embedded within operational processes.

In small and medium firms, those processes are simpler than in larger structures and rely on people who simply know each other and work together.

Developing an inner knowledge of the organisation and its culture is always going to be key for the CISO in small firms, and it will definitely be harder to establish if the role is externalised and delivered on a part-time basis or remotely. At best, it could take a long time to deliver value; at worse, it could simply become useless.

Finally, organisations deciding to take that route must also consider the portfolio of other clients their externalised CISO would be supporting. This is absolutely essential to avoid conflicts of interests – for example up and down the supply chain – and the risk of confidentiality breaches – for example towards competitors.

Overall, beyond any cynical "box-checking" and before jumping to ready-made conclusions, small and medium firms should consider the following questions to determine the type of CISO they need:

- What's their initial level of cybersecurity maturity?

- What's their ambition in terms of maturity development?

- In which regulatory framework do they operate? And how is it likely to evolve over the short to mid-term?

- What is the level of cybersecurity maturity of the supply chain or the ecosystem around them?

- What are the levels of cybersecurity expectations of their customers, partners or investors?

It's only by looking at their own cybersecurity context in that way that they will be able to right-size and position a CISO role which will work for them.

#65 A Real-life Take on the Cyber Security Skills Gap[1]

17 September 2020

The security industry must rebuild its narrative to attract more raw talent at all levels

You don't have to go far these days to find security professionals complaining about skills shortages, and countless media outlets relaying their views.

But there are at least two sides to this argument and the situation requires a more balanced approach.

There is no doubt – first of all – that the cyber security industry still has an image problem. It often carries a dated tech-heavy narrative and ends up being perceived as an obscure and complex technical niche, something reserved to nerds and geeks: When the excellent ladies of the CEFCYS in Paris published their first guide to the cyber security professions earlier this year, they titled it "I don't wear a hoodie, yet I work in cyber security"... ("Je ne porte pas de sweat à capuche, pourtant je travaille dans la cybersécurité"[2])

In fact, the security industry has never managed to make itself attractive and in turn, the lack of awareness around the diversity of security roles breeds a lack of relevant training courses and educational opportunities.

The absence of clear security career paths is also a real problem at all levels when it comes to attract new talent: What do you do once you have been a security analyst in a SOC for a few years? (or a CISO for that matter?) ... you should not have to be condemned to hopping across to similar roles all the times, but credible alternative role models are cruelly missing: How many CISOs have actually become CIO? or COO, or CRO?

---

1 You can watch JC Gaillard talk through the content of this article at the Cyber Security Leadership Summit 2020 on 10th November 2020 on the Corix Partners YouTube channel > https://www.youtube.com/watch?v=THh1Z_TLZcQ

2 https://www.amazon.fr/porte-capuche-pourtant-travaille-cybersécurité/dp/2749601622

However, this is rarely what people refer to when they talk about the "cyber security skills gap" …

They often refer to problems in staffing large security initiatives or security operations centres, and here the so-called skills gap is often a fig leaf hiding different problems.

Many security leaders – in particular in large organisations – are stuck with legacy operational processes – around identity management, security monitoring, incident handling or threat intelligence – which are mostly manual, labour-intensive, repetitive and built around countless tools (20 on average according to a recent Cisco report[3]). Attracting – and retaining – young professionals in such jobs can indeed be hard – even harder in absence of clear career paths and role models as we highlighted above.

Also many large organisations, faced with large scale maturity problems and urgent security transformation challenges, are trying – unrealistically – to fix all their problems at the same time. But building a monstrous programme of work requiring in theory tens of additional FTEs, and ignoring all dependencies between tasks and cultural aspects, is not how you change things. You would struggle to staff it in any specialised industry – and to deliver it. This is just bad planning, and it is fuelled by the tech industry and large consultancies.

So does all this reflect a real shortage of skills? or a shortage of appetite from the leadership to tackle the re-engineering of legacy security processes, to make them attractive and better suited to the expectations of a younger workforce? or is the alleged shortage of skills simply an excuse to hide poor management and the greed of the security ecosystem?

Ultimately, all those aspects are just the different sides of the same problem: To attract more raw talent into the security industry (at all levels, security management included), you have to make it more attractive, in a credible and meaningful way – at all levels.

---

3 See https://www.securitymagazine.com/articles/91776-cisco-2020-ciso-benchmark-report
  -average-company-uses-20-security-technologies

To help with that at analyst level, the leadership should focus on decluttering the cyber security estates and automating processes intelligently to allow a smaller number of analysts to work more efficiently, creating a more stimulating – and less boring – environment for them.

At middle and senior level, the focus should be on building role models and career paths, showcasing real, meaningful and credible bridges across cyber security roles and other roles, at least across the broader GRC spectrum, but ideally across the entire management spectrum. Looking beyond tech is absolutely key in that space. There is no reason why a CISO would not come from a business role.

Professional bodies and industry bodies have a role to play here to rebuild that narrative and help the security industry become more attractive and move forward.

These are the themes I have been exploring with the techUK Cyber Security team and which have been summarised in this report[4] released in December 2020.

4 https://www.techuk.org/resource/techuk-launches-the-ciso-at-the-c-suite-report.html

#66 Cyber Security Automation is Key to Fight the Skills Gap

29 April 2021

To start building solutions to the skills gap problem, it is key to look at it in all its dimensions.

The debate around the cyber security skills gap continues to ride fairly high on the security industry's agenda, but to start building solutions, it is key to look at the problem in all its dimensions.

The cyber security skills gap problem has its origins in three interlocking factors:

There is undoubtedly a growing demand for cyber skills, rooted in long-term trends towards the digitization of many industries and the avalanche of cyber-attacks we have seen over the past 10 years, both aspects greatly amplified by the COVID crisis.

Many organisations – large and small – which never had an infosec function before now have one or are building one. Many organisations which didn't know what a pen test was are now doing those regularly. We need far more cyber security analysts, developers, testers, managers than ever before; and education and training programmes are struggling to keep up with the growth of the demand and the diversity of the roles.

But you cannot end the analysis at this point and conclude that the solution lies entirely in attracting and training more people. Because the problem has at least two additional dimensions you also need to act on:

Many large organisations tend to respond to the growing cyber security emergency by scaling up legacy operational processes and with the perpetuation of a culture which believes that the solution of all cyber security problems is technical in nature and requires more tools. This is fuelled by countless tech vendors and large consultancies, but also by many CISOs being technologists by trade and by background and hopping from job to job, carrying with them the same technical recipes. This has led to a proliferation of tools – poorly integrated, often partially deployed or implemented – which simply embeds manual steps within security operational processes in many large firms and dramatically increases their demand for resources and skills.

This is also attritive in nature, in particular at analyst level and in many entry-level cyber security roles because it results in jobs which are excessively repetitive and boring, with limited career development options. So, attracting and training more people is key to fixing the cyber security skills gap – certainly in the long run – but if you can't keep them in the industry because you give them boring jobs to do and no career path, this has the potential to become a self-perpetuating problem.

To break this cycle, and in parallel to increasing long-term efforts around training at all levels, the security industry must look at the mid to short-term, accelerate on automation and tools integration and focus on decluttering legacy tooling landscapes and operational processes, to give fewer analysts more exciting jobs where they can develop more and bring more value.

It is certainly more difficult for CISOs than just hiring more people but jumping straight at AI-driven solutions – which may be immature or over-hyped – is not the answer either, but just the continuation of the same tech-driven obsession which has led to the proliferation of security tools in the first place.

More than ever, the key to drive a successful decluttering and automation project around cyber security is to keep things simple and focus on people and process first, then technology.

#67 A few big hacks in the US and everybody is talking about ransomware again...

17 June 2021

Defence in depth is key, but why are we hearing so little about it? Time for a few hard truths

Frankly, this is starting to become embarrassing for some security professionals. In these columns, we have been writing about ransomware since 2016, and even at the time, it was reasonably established as a topic and already a subject of events and conferences. We revisited it in 2019 in the light of an event in Paris targeted at SMBs, in which we participated. Since then, it has grown monumentally and its impact has increased even further with the pandemic; now even cyber insurers are starting to change their tune about it…

Meanwhile, some in the security community continue to go round in circles, looking for straight answers or technical silver bullets: Should you pay the ransom? … Is it all about backups? …

It's time for a few hard truths.

The debate around paying – or not paying – the ransom is typical of the confusion that reigns, amplified by increasingly contrasted messages from public authorities – who seem to be resisting making ransom payments illegal – and cyber insurers – who might have played an ambiguous game in the recent past.

There is no "Robin Hood" story line here; this is not about robbing the rich to feed the poor: Paying ransoms finances organised crime. Period. Paying or not should be a reasonably plain matter of business ethics.

Let's consider the following scenario, as a matter of comparison:

You are the CEO of a business which has been heavily affected by the COVID crisis; you were not in an ideal shape pre-COVID and competition was already hitting hard at you; you have struggled to keep going and find finance throughout the crisis; you literally have a few months of runway ahead of you, before having to have a difficult discussion with creditors, possibly leading to the lay off people in big numbers.

An opportunity presents itself to open a new market in an emerging country; it is a solid opportunity and you have been aware of it for years, but you have stayed away from it; access to the market involves paying large sums to corrupt officials, in a regime which is openly recognised by international agencies as being involved in drug and people trafficking.

What do you do?

My point is simply: You must see the debate around ransomware and the payment of ransoms in the same ethical light, because ransomware is cybercrime; it is deluded to see paying the ransom as some form of economic trade-off and a regular business transaction...

Now, everybody can understand that it is a hard decision to make when your business is actually down, but it should still be guided by ethical considerations and an increased level of support of public authorities towards the victims; something we were already pushing for in 2019 in support of small businesses.

Making ransom payments illegal without adequately supporting victims could make things worse, as the Cyber Threat Alliance rightly argues.

Having said that, protecting yourself can be hard, especially if you are just waking up to the problem now, well passed the 11th hour...

There is no silver bullet. Period.

The only thing that can protect you is defence in depth, and it could take years to put it in place properly at the level of a large enterprise if you're truly starting now.

* Yes, you need to educate your staff around phishing and opening up attachments ... but by itself, that's not enough ... human mistakes are unavoidable ...

* Yes, you need to filter emails upstream to remove any suspicious content ... but by itself, that's not enough ... some might still go through ...

- Yes, you need to deploy security patches in a timely manner across your entire estate … but by itself, that's not enough … you will always miss a few across large estates …

- Yes, you need to take and maintain regular backups, so that you can return to business quickly … but by itself, that's not enough … by then, the deed is done, and your business has been affected … and by the way, the life of most CIOs is full of backups that didn't work …

You need to act in a concerted manner across all those levels, and many others, to achieve true protection: This is not just about having a rehearsed incident response plan ready, with lawyers and PR people lined up …

Cynically, many recent ransomware incidents are challenging in a harsh way the way security has been prioritised in many industry sectors over the years, and how the focus on technology, point-solutions, and low hanging fruits fails to protect the large enterprise in real terms.

This cannot be reduced to a matter of insufficient investments: Large firms have spent billions collectively on cyber security over the past decades; it's an excessive focus on pure tech solutions coupled with execution failure, which is at the heart of the situation many organisations are now facing.

This is also a challenge for some CISOs – and tech vendors and large consultancies – who would have effectively accepted and endorsed the "risk appetite" decision of business leaders, unwilling to understand and challenge the fact that this is actually driven by cognitive biases, that "risk appetite" goes out of the window at the first sight of real problems, and that there cannot be a proper discussion around "risk appetite" without a genuine appreciation of the threats targeting the business, and the protective measures the business has in place – or not – to protect itself from those threats.

The hard truth is that good practices – known for decades – can still protect against ransomware if properly deployed – in layers – across the real breadth and depth of the modern enterprise.

True defence in depth is complex; it requires a coherent vision, the right governance and operating model, and the right skills at the right level across the enterprise; but it simply works at creating a protective shield: Siloed vision and point tech solutions don't.

#68 The Problem with Cyber Security ROI

5 August 2021

CISOs being asked those questions should look beyond the topic itself and face the underlying issues it might be hiding.

If the reporting line of the CISO is the oldest ongoing topic of discussion amongst cyber security communities, security ROI is probably the second oldest…

In reality, it hides several endemic problems which have been plaguing the security industry for the last two decades.

First of all, it downgrades cyber security to a mere matter of investments — that would have to be justified — implying that lack of funding and lack of resources are at the heart of low security maturity levels and the cyber-attacks epidemic we have been seeing for the last 10 years.

In fact, problems have largely been elsewhere: Large organisations have committed billions collectively to cyber security over the period; it's governance and cultural issues which have led to adverse prioritisation and execution failure.

While it might be the case that some organisations have not invested enough in relation to the threats they face, the security ROI discussions are often the sign of arbitrary programmes of work driven bottom-up by a CISO, either replicating recipes applied elsewhere or listening to the sirens of some tech vendors, when not simply pushing their own pet projects.

Cyber security did not appear overnight with the COVID pandemic. Any large organisations will have a history and a legacy of some sort in that space spanning two decades.

Understanding the investments made in the past, what has worked, what hasn't (and the reasons why), and showing decision makers that lessons are being learnt around past execution failures would be more important to build trust than a financial ROI calculation which will be invariably plagued by disputable assumptions and estimates, leaving it vulnerable to internal politics and horse trading around numbers.

Because very often, trust — or the lack of it — is at the heart of the context here, in particular when the ROI question comes top-down onto the CISO. Many CISOs take it as a normal business question and a natural justification to give, while in fact it tends to mean "I am not sure I understand what you are trying to do and why you want to spend so much".

It is a rare concern at the top these days, in the face of non-stop cyber-attacks and data breaches; boards are often more concerned with demonstrating they are spending enough on cyber.

So the persistence of the cyber security ROI debates is to be seen in my view as a symptom of the distrust and the lack of positive engagement between the CISO and senior stakeholders, and a defence mechanism on their part.

Any large organisation would have spent millions or tens of millions — if not more — on cyber security over the past decades; you cannot blame senior execs for being suspicious when they see in front of them yet another investment plan in that space…

Instead of jumping straight into a financial ROI debate where they are likely to lose credit, CISOs who want to drive large-scale transformative programmes around cyber security, should focus first on building trust with senior stakeholders and solid communication channels with all of them, working across silos towards business units, geographies and support functions such as Legal, HR or Procurement, as well as IT and their suppliers.

Even if they are working towards the delivery of a long-term large-scale roadmap, they should split it into cheaper manageable chunks, to demonstrate their execution capabilities with simple achievable tasks, addressing business expectations, before getting to meatier (and more expensive) matters.

By then, their own clarity of vision and their ability to execute should carry them sufficiently to avoid arbitrary — and often useless — discussions around ROI.

That's the key with discussions around cyber security ROI: They shouldn't be happening at all in the current context, given the non-stop avalanche of cyber-attacks we are seeing world-wide.

CISOs being asked those questions should look beyond the topic itself and face the underlying issues it might be hiding.

The First
100 Days
of the
New CISO

#69 The First 100 Days of the New CISO

15 March 2018 [with Vincent Viers]

There is some form of management reality beyond the "100 days" journalistic cliché: How does an incoming executive make an impact in a new role? What are the real timeframes to look at, and what can be expected and over what horizon? What are the key issues that should raise a red flag during the first few months in a new senior position? and those which can be ignored?

Those are the themes we have been exploring on the Corix Partners blog since November 2017 around the specific role of the incoming CISO.

Of course, each and everyone's own path to success will ultimately depend on the specific context of their arrival — from their own previous experience at this level of responsibilities to the firm's security management maturity. We believe, however, that this series of articles will prove helpful in guiding most CISOs through their first steps in a new organisation and provide them with a useful roadmap about making an impact in their new job.

Our experience drives us to split the new CISO's roadmap into 3 different time horizons which can be roughly encapsulated into a 6-days / 6-weeks / 6-month paradigm. These three milestones represent good opportunities for the incoming CISO to focus on what truly matters at each step— and to highlight what they should not yet be concerned about.

It is key – in our opinion – for any new CISO to hit the ground running so your first six days should be dedicated to start engaging actively with your direct management and with your staff. As much as possible, you must meet with them face-to-face to start building a stronger personal bond. Make use of those first interactions to understand how reporting lines work in your new organization (upwards, downwards and sideways across matrix models), to position the challenge ahead and to identify key preexisting roadblocks. The only thing that should worry you at this point should be the inability to properly schedule those key first meetings because stakeholders don't have time for you. Now would also be a good time to get the finance question straight: Do you have a budget allocated and how is it managed? Without appropriate resources, you won't be able to achieve much.

Your first six weeks should be the natural continuity of the first six days. Only by meeting as many relevant stakeholders as possible will you be able to accurately assess the situation you are inheriting of as a CISO. Key at this stage is to listen, listen and listen instead of coming up with ready-made solutions, or focusing only on the burning fires. Travel if you must and take time to gather your thoughts, then start drafting a strategic framework — ameliorative directions, time-frames, and high-level costs — to address your findings, in relation to the objectives and challenges identified during your first week. Your main objective around this time should be to get your strategic framework validated with your boss, but you should be fully prepared if your plan is properly costed, rooted in tangible field observations and the expectations of key stakeholders. Lack of engagement from your management beyond merely tactical and technical topics and a general lack of interest from stakeholders for a truly transformative agenda should raise red flags.

Once validated, the next step must consist of executing your strategic framework and it will start with the formal setting up of an appropriate governance and operating model, as well as getting as many senior team members and stakeholders on board as you can. You should now be getting ready to implement what is very likely to be a mid- to long-term plan, and you must resist being pushed or drawn into tactical firefighting. Focus on infusing a sense of clarity among all stakeholders, both about timing and objectives.

As it turns out, your sixth month in the job should correspond approximately to your first 100 (working) days, and it is a good time to start looking back on your journey while recognizing that you are really only getting started.

While a 100 days framework is a useful model to think about getting up to speed in your new role, you must keep in mind that any lasting change in an organization's InfoSec practices is likely to require steady work over a period of several years.

So while this series of articles should help you hit the ground running, always keep in mind that, if your objectives are rooted in delivering lasting change around cybersecurity, you are in for a marathon, not a sprint.

#70 The Person, the Role and the Culture of the Firm

2 November 2017

There is some form of management reality beyond the "100 days" journalistic cliché: How does an incoming executive make an impact in a new role? What are the real timeframes to look at? What can be expected, and over what horizon? What are the key issues that should raise a red flag during the first few months in a new senior position? and those which can be ignored? Those are the themes we will be exploring in this new series around the specific role of the CISO.

The Person, the Role and the Culture of the Firm

It is alas necessary to start this series by a long list of caveats and questions: Every person is different, every organisation is different and to a large extent, every CISO role is also different.

Although we will be identifying common trends in the coming articles — looking in turn at the first 6 days, 6 weeks and 6 months of the incoming CISO — they must be understood and placed by the reader in their specific personal context and in the specific context of their organisation. In particular, the heterogeneity in maturity levels among firms in terms of security management must be acknowledged.

The following guiding questions are key for each reader to relate the series to their personal frame of mind:

- Is this your first CISO job? What were you doing before? Are you coming into this from an IT background or not?

- Is this your second CISO job? What happened in the first one? Why did you leave? How long did you stay?

- Is this your third CISO job (or more)? (then why are you reading this?)

- Is this an internal move? Upwards? Sideways? Or are you joining a new firm?

- What are your expectations with the new job? Was it a real positive decision to move into Security? Or just a holding pattern waiting for better things to emerge? Was the decision made for you? (were you pushed into this? did you have a choice?) Was it a political calculation? ("Security people don't get sacked")

- What motivates you? Building teams? Managing people? Doing stuff?

- What are your timeframes with regards to the new position? How long do you see yourself staying in the job? What would be your next job after this one? Is your career something you care about and actively build? or do you take a more passive approach to career-building?

The above is not just an endless HR checklist, but the real context in which each reader should place this series.

The CISO role is not just another senior management role: It can be an extremely complex and transversal position, where you may be expected to articulate security concepts from the Board down across all layers of the enterprise, juggling between technical and business terms while always remaining credible.

You will have to deal with data breaches one day and compliance problems the next, while battling with cognitive or emotional biases at managerial level above you and besides you. You may feel exposed or vulnerable.

Your reporting line, the personality of your boss, the skills and structure of the team you inherit – if any – will only be pieces of a much bigger jigsaw. In large firms, you will be immersed in a complex political game across the GRC galaxy, in a context where the "three-lines-of-defence" model is rarely applied in its purest form, and sometimes poorly understood. And there may be international or multi-cultural aspects to contend with as well.

All that in the specific security maturity context of each organisation. A context that will vary from firm to firm and will be the sum – for better or worse – of all your predecessors' actions as well as countless management decisions around the security space spanning the best part of the last 20 years.

Those decisions and attitudes will have created a culture around security that the incoming CISO needs to grasp quickly, because everything they do or say during their first few months will be seen internally through that prism.

Unsurprisingly, listening will be key throughout that phase until all challenges are clearly positioned and the new CISO can start articulating a strategic framework to address those challenges and then a model for its execution.

Those are the topics we will be exploring in the next articles in this series.

#71 The First Week: The Firm and its People: Positioning the Challenge

16 November 2017

Many of the management tips we will be building up in this series could apply to any executive taking up a senior job in a new organisation. But the role of the CISO is particularly sensitive in many aspects and has its own dynamics. It is often poorly understood by management and still seen by some as a necessary evil, or as an imposition by auditors or regulators. Even where threats are understood and the need to protect the firm against cybercrime is on the Board's agenda, what the role exactly entails is not always clear for all stakeholders (as may be the case for a CFO or Head of HR position). So the need to effectively engage all parties from the start is key for the new CISO.

The Month Before

Your first week in the new job starts a long time before you arrive. You'll need to understand the true nature of the new business you're getting into, its culture, its geographical footprint, and all the aspects that will help you "hit the ground running".

It should involve true and solid homework, but more importantly, you must try to network with ex-colleagues and contacts who work or have worked there and get as much insider information as you can

Expect the first few months to be hard work: Not all firms are well managed, and you cannot expect security to be well managed in a firm that isn't. Likewise, you cannot expect good security governance where corporate governance is poor. You might have been hired to "sort security out". Do not expect this to be easy.

6 Days (the first week): The Firm and its People: Positioning the Challenge

Bosses

You need to have a clear understanding of your reporting line and meet with your direct boss face to face (NOT REMOTELY) straight away. Personal interactions are key in senior roles and you'll have to develop a direct and strong relationship and personal bond with your line management. Those things are rarely built up over conference calls.

In large firms where you may have to contend with a matrix organisation and a functional manager, you need to meet with them too and understand how the matrix model really works. You'll need to gauge the relative strength of each matrixial direction, and whether they complement or antagonise each other. If your functional boss is not based where you are, you should at least speak to them during your first week, then immediately schedule a trip to visit them.

You must hear from your management directly in their own words what the true dominant challenge of your role is: Build a security practice? Rebuild it? Run it? Optimise it? Transfer it to another part of the organisation? What happened to the person previously occupying your role? What amount of legacy do you have to deal with and what is the perception your management has of it?

Those first meetings must be clear, open, and unencumbered on all sides. Crucially, they must happen straight away.

You should schedule periodic meetings with your management at the same time. A monthly frequency is probably best to start with. It will give you an immediate target to work against (i.e. your next meeting with them). Those meetings do not need a fixed agenda to start with as it is obvious that you will be on a discovery and planning phase for a while.

Of course, you would have been told all sort of things throughout your hiring process and you would have gathered your own "intelligence" about your new organisation as part of your own preparation phase, but now you will start to see it from the inside: You will need to assess the politics and the rules of internal power, understand your bosses' reporting line, the overall structure of the team you a part of and the key players around you, as well as the current structure of your own team (if you have one).

Staff

If you have a team structured under you, you should of course meet with all your team members in due course (size permitting), starting immediately with your own direct reports. You should meet face to face with all those who are based where you are, and speak to all the others. More than mere introductory opportunities, those meetings are the ideal vehicle to gauge personalities and hear grievances. It obviously goes both ways and your staff will forge their "first impression" of you through those meetings. Don't talk too much. Simply ask them what they expect from you and listen to them.

There will be a fine line not to cross as you must not give them the sense that you are committing to fix all their problems (which may or may not be well founded, and you're unlikely to have all the facts to be judge of that). Expect politics may be played and some may try to test you. Worry not: You will get a lot more of that in the weeks to come...

Money

During this first week, you also need to identify the budget you have (if any) and how it is managed. You should meet with your departmental Finance team and understand straight away where you stand with regard to the current and next budget cycles: How much was your department allocated in the last budget? How much has been consumed? What are the rules to authorise spending? What is your signing limit (if any)? When does the next budgetary cycle start and when are the next budgetary submissions due?

Without autonomous resources, you'll be dependent on others. This is a key aspect to address upfront.

That's quite a lot to cram into a few days, but should you achieve it, you'll be off to a good start.

The key things to worry about in the first week (which should raise a red flag because they concern the real profile of your new role and management priorities)

- Your direct boss hasn't got time to meet with you.

- You are not allowed to schedule travel to meet your functional boss on ground of costs.

- You haven't got a proper budget, or cannot identify the right Finance team to talk to.

The things NOT to worry about in the first week (which are just management opportunities for you to address)

- Your direct boss cannot articulate clearly his priorities with regards to your role.

- Your functional boss is OK to meet you but didn't know you had been hired.

- Your own direct reports do not open up and you do not learn much from meeting them.

#72 The Six Weeks Horizon: The Firm and its Management: Defining and validating a Strategic Framework

30 November 2017

This is really the time-horizon over which the new CISO must start assessing their new position. Once again, many of the management tips we will be building up in this series could apply to any executive taking up a senior job in a new organisation. But the CISO role is often a complex transversal role; It is easy to get disheartened, particularly in large organisations, and indeed it becomes relevant to start paying attention if red flags start accumulating two months into the job.

At this stage, you should have started to get a feel for the organisation you have entered, and you would have established first contacts with key team members and your direct management.

You need to continue to meet with your team members, preferably face to face whenever possible. You should meet each team member, if the size and geographical dispersion of your team allows, even if it's just for a very short introduction. Do not hint at any possible organisational changes, even if you start to sense that some will have to eventually take place.

If you identify personal or HR issues, consult with your direct line management and take guidance before jumping into action: Many of those issues are often rooted in a past that might be more complex that what was disclosed to you by the employee… If necessary, you should meet with the HR department, but only when in possession of all the relevant facts.

Expect that your team members (and others as you continue to meet people) will start bringing "problems" to you and will "test" you: That's a good and natural reaction and you must play along: it is key for them to get to know you and to gauge your management style. At the same time, you have only been in the job for a few weeks and cannot make miracles (they must understand that, too).

Expect as well that many people will tell you what needs fixing, how to do it and why it hasn't been done in the past. That is also unavoidable and a good sign. It will invariably bring a mix of real value and political noise, but you must listen to it.

Overall this is an opportunity for you to get to know the people around you, but you must not allow the short-term firefighting dynamics to take over: You need to continue discovering the true extent of your environment and meeting with key stakeholders around you outside your team should be the real backbone of those first six weeks.

You should identify primarily from the meetings with your staff who your key stakeholders are across the firm, and who are the key external third-parties and suppliers in your environment.

Apply the same approach you used for the meetings you held during your first week: Ask people what they expect from you, how you can help them, and more importantly listen to them.

Do not hesitate to travel during that phase, in particular if your organisation has a large multi-national footprint. Travelling will introduce a different rhythm of work and may help you gather your thoughts.

In all cases, start organising the notes and observations you would have accumulated throughout your first few weeks and building your own assessment of the situation you have inherited. The focus of that first assessment will depend to a large extent on the key challenge of your role, as defined by your management and positioned during your first week:

Fig. 12: Focus of the new CISO first assessment

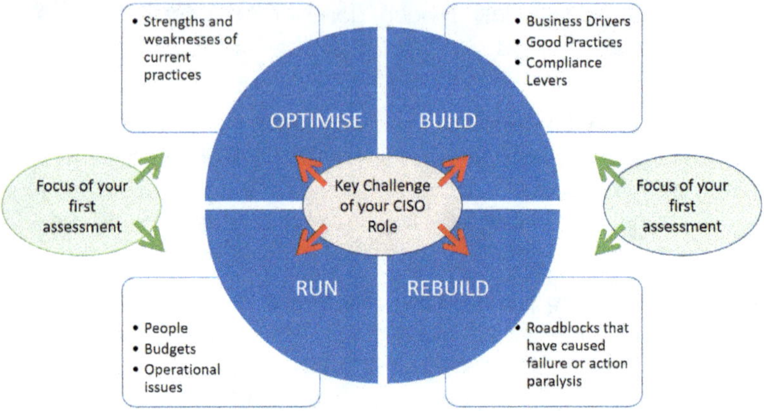

Your strategic framework should express in simple terms what you want to do to address the challenge given to you. It should reflect the key findings of your assessment, and set directions, timeframes and high-level costs estimates for what you are proposing to achieve in response to your findings.

Make all necessary caveats around unknown aspects, and if necessary, offer multiple ameliorative options or action paths.

Trust your instincts, look over the right timeframes in terms of execution and do not focus only on alleged "quick wins". There are things that can be done in six months and some that may take a year or two to be completed, depending on the complexity of your environment.

Most importantly, do not hint at organisational changes at this stage, even if your meetings so far have made it clear to you that some will have to take place. That should come next as a matter of execution of the strategic framework once agreed.

Share your strategic framework with your direct reports once advanced enough: Collect their feedback and make the necessary amendments, then take it to your boss for validation.

That validation meeting with your boss is really the objective you should have been working towards across the whole period. You should not fear it and if you have followed the approach highlighted here, you should have all the facts and the confidence to sail through it. Your case should be as strong as it can be, as long as it is clear, simple, rooted in the reality of your field observations and aligned with the challenges given to you.

The key things to worry about in the first 6 weeks (which should raise a red flag because they concern the real profile of your new role and management priorities)

- You are struggling to meet stakeholders; they say they haven't got time to meet you

- Stakeholders openly reject any form of value proposition from you that steps beyond tactical firefighting

- You still haven't got any form of clarity around budgets and nobody wants to talk to you about it; you have missed key budgetary deadlines and you will have to wait until the next round

The things NOT to worry about in the first 6 weeks (which are just management opportunities for you to address)

- Stakeholders don't seem to understand what you say

- Your team members don't seem to understand what you say

- You come across serious operational issues or acute immaturity problems that go way beyond what you were told or what you were expecting

#73 The 6 Months Horizon: The Firm and its Culture: Defining and validating an Execution Framework

18 January 2018

This is the point when you really get stuck in. By now, you would have been in the new CISO job for about 2 months and it should start to feel less and less like a new job. Of course, this is not really about 100 days, and you should also start to realise it.

Over the past 6 weeks, you would have met with your management and your team. You would have met with key stakeholders around you and developed a sense of the challenges ahead, including the cultural and geographical diversity of your new organisation. You would have built a sense of what needs to be done, where you are in terms of budgetary cycle and the resources you have or could claim to deliver. You would have consolidated all that into a strategic framework that you would have presented back to your management, taking into account their objectives for your role, and the expectations of all stakeholders. It would have been hard work and it probably feels like you have already been there for a long time. You are ready to go.

At this point, we have to assume that your management has broadly accepted your assessment of the situation, and the approach you proposed to move forward. If that's not the case, you need to examine the points of divergence and decide the best course of action. If those are too salient, you should leave. Period. Everybody can make a mistake, and this is probably best for all parties if those issues are highlighted early on. If you believe there is still room for maneuver and the adjustments are positive, you should play on. This is for you to judge and no-one else.

If you stay on, the first thing you need to put in place at this stage, is the governance model that will carry you through the execution of your strategic framework.

It needs to fit within the organisation around you and you must start by understanding the structure of existing management committees, their membership and terms of reference. You will need a senior security management committee to supervise your strategic delivery and arbitrate on conflicts, but you must avoid excessive and useless committee duplication. It needs to be chaired by the most senior stakeholder you can convince, ideally a board member and your bosses' boss. This is key to showcase the importance and value of security for the firm. You should draw on the contacts with stakeholders built up during your first weeks to identify the people who are the most likely to help you move forward, and you must not compromise on the seniority of the membership. Schedule the first committee meeting as soon as possible. This is your true starting point. An overview of your strategic framework and high-level timeframes should offer a natural agenda. Their formal endorsement of your objectives and their ongoing oversight will be the backbone against which all your actions will rest.

In parallel, you need to build the target operating model that will support your strategic delivery. This is entirely dependent on your strategic objectives in terms of content and structure, but it needs to be clear and simple. This is to some extent related to your reporting line, and very likely to be influenced by your relationship – personal and functional – with the CIO.

You will need to validate the target operating model with your management, your senior team members, and key stakeholders. Depending on your corporate employment culture and the extent of the changes you are proposing, you may need to consult with the HR department. In turn, you may need to involve employee representatives or workers councils. It will take time, which is why you need to get this started as soon as possible and keep it as clear and simple as possible. This is also why you need the backing of the most senior executives you can gather around your project.

It needs to be a mid- to long-term move rooted in your strategic assessment of the situation you found and aligned with your transformation objectives over the same time horizons.

Once all is agreed, align the structure of your own team, update job descriptions, performance metrics and where necessary salaries and compensation levels at the first opportunity. You may need to hire and – maybe – fire, which will also take time and efforts. Another reason to get to this point as quickly as you can.

It should now be clear that this period of several months following the conclusion of your assessment phase, should be about installing the execution framework that will carry your strategic delivery plan.

During that phase, you must stay focused on your mid- to long-term management objectives and resist being drawn or pushed into tactical delivery. There may be urgent issues requiring your time and attention, or incidents to deal with, but they are just that — tactical diversions. They are not what you are here for. You are here to deliver the strategic framework agreed upon with your management and the senior security committee.

At the same time, set expectations at the right level: True and lasting change takes "the time it takes" and it is irremediably killed by short-termist flip-flopping. If you need to deviate tactically from your long-term goals, make it clear this is only tactical and temporary and in due course get back on track. Make it clear to all stakeholders that you will stay in the job for the time it takes: That's the true "secret sauce" to real and lasting transformation.

And now, get things underway: Clarity should be there over what needs to be done, by whom and over what timeframes. Keep things simple, break them down into small chunks as much as you can and get them done one after another. That's the only way to "eat an elephant" as the old joke goes…

The key things to worry about in the first 6 months (which should raise a red flag because they concern the real profile of your new role and management priorities)

- You cannot attract or retain the right senior stakeholders at the security management committee, in particular as the chairperson

- Organisational rigidity and HR constraints prevent you from making the necessary adjustments to your team

- Tactical firefighting is still the only thing stakeholders around you associate with security (instead of the structured and pro-active protection of the business from real threats)

The things NOT to worry about in the first 6 months (which are just management opportunities for you to address)

- Progress is slow

- You lose more team members than expected (or some you didn't want to lose)

- Fundamental business changes (mergers, acquisitions) seem to disrupt everything around you (those are often the best times to drive real transformation)

#74 The Transformational CISO: Making an impact and driving change... and what happens beyond the 6 months horizon

1 February 2018

Through this series, we have examined how an incoming CISO can create the conditions to truly make a difference in their new job.

Of course, as we stated in the introductory article , all companies are different from one another and so are most individuals. Each will be at their particular stage in terms of security or managerial maturity.

But beyond the journalistic "100 days" cliché, there is real and strong management common sense in having the objective of making a real impact over a 6 months horizon (which is not so far from 120 – business – days after all !!!).

The CISO role, irrespective of its actual exact content and reporting line, will always be peculiar: It is not a true C-suite role, and security topics can have the tendency to scare senior executives who associate them with problems and costs.

So creating a strong bond of trust with all stakeholders will be key to the success of the new CISO. This will come through patient listening, the development of a clear vision, achievable transformation objectives over realistic timeframes, and a sense of leadership which puts clarity, simplicity and consistency at the core of your daily work.

We have said it repeatedly in earlier articles: This is a complex role which requires extensive management experience, personal gravitas, political acumen and a solid grasp of the internal workings of an organisation (particularly in large firms). It requires the real field experience of a battle-hardened professional. This is not a job for an ex-auditor or a life-long consultant.

Staying the course will also be paramount: In essence, what gets mapped out and put under way at the end of the first 6 months is a first cycle of work.

It will now have to be delivered and it is likely to be a multi-year effort. Management acumen, staff focus, and budgetary resources will have to be sustained. Tactical disruptions will have to be handled. The whole show will have to stay on the road and success will have to be sold.

To achieve real and lasting change, the CISO must not leave at the end of this first cycle but stay through the transition period that will follow, map out, and drive – or at least supervise – the following cycle. True and lasting transformation will come out of that second cycle of change, as the impact of the first one gets accepted and stakeholders start getting used to working differently with a security practice that is coherent and brings value.

Once the initial vision has been established and stabilised, it will have to be optimised. Each of these cycles – creation, stabilisation, optimisation – could last 2 to 3 years in any complex organisation. So, the real tenure of the transformational CISO has to be considered on a 6 to 9 years horizon, and certainly nothing much shorter if the change objectives are to be lasting and fundamental.

It is a very significant commitment for the CISO, who will have to be rewarded and incentivised to stay the course. It will also be very significant for its management and many organisations are simply incapable of thinking over such a long-term horizon. But those which can will reap the rewards and build for themselves a true security culture that can only be a competitive advantage in today's world.

So, 6 days, 6 weeks, 6 months, 6 years… Beyond 100 days, here is probably the real timeline to consider for the transformational CISO.

#75 First 100 Days of the New CISO: How to avoid the "Curse of Firefighting"?

2 August 2018 [with Vincent Viers]

Constant firefighting downgrades the role and the CISO must fight to avoid its gravitational pull

With regards to many other C-level roles, the Chief Information Security Officer (CISO) position is a fairly recent creation for many organisations. Although it started to emerge over 15 years ago, it has been spurred further recently by growing concerns over cybersecurity and highly publicized data breaches. Figuring out its right place within organisations is still quite a hot debate between management and security experts

How an incoming executive needs to approach such a complex role is also a hot debate. Many experts – including us – have written about this and have framed the topic using the "first 100 days" journalistic cliché. In our own series, we took issue with the fact that most consultants' analysis and suggestions fail to consider the incoming CISO within the broader context and organisational complexity of the firm.

In large organisations, no function exists in a vacuum, and getting anything done requires aligning your strategy with other stakeholders' priorities, business cycles, and budget cycles. It will always take time, as well as political and managerial acumen, but nothing in our opinion that could not be set in motion to an extent with the first 6 months in office.

In practice, the real challenge always lies in balancing strategic longer-term views with the tactical aspects of the day-to-day of the function: It is unavoidable that an amount of time during the CISO's first months in the job will be spent dealing with tactical firefighting and that it will impact their ability to elevate to the level required to start weighing in on key strategic issues.

As one of our contributors pointed out – a CISO at a large services organisation – "the 100 days often end around day 3".

There is no way around this: If you want to stay in place in this kind of role for more than 100 days, you must deal with the day-to-day emergencies; you must meet expectations before you can transcend them.

This is especially true when the CISO reports directly to the CIO – which often results in concentrating the role on its most technical dimensions and is accentuated further by the short-termist culture of many IT executives.

It is a context where it is easy for the CISO to be tempted to give up and think that tactical issues will always win and will prevent the role from ever elevating beyond mere firefighting. Even worse for organisations, this situation is often self-perpetuating: A tactical mindset breeds tactical attitudes, and short-termism is hard to escape once you start indulging in it.

Taking this somewhat fatalistic view to its logical conclusion, it becomes the type of situation where the positioning of the CISO within the organisation is bound to evolve and move under a CSO type-of-position whose responsibility would be to elevate the transversal topic of cybersecurity to address the more and more pressing questions from the board and senior stakeholders on these matters.

This would leave the CISO with the downscaled but unambiguous task of dealing with the day-to-day firefighting aspects of the function, while it becomes the role of the CSO to push strategic cybersecurity initiatives throughout the organisation.

While in our opinion the emergence of CSO roles is unavoidable in many large organisations due to the increasing pressure on boards around cyber security matters, and the emergence of broader transversal topics such as resilience or privacy, it is achievable for the CISO to elevate their position to a highly strategic and respected level, but it will require strong managerial acumen and personal gravitas to know how to deal with the tactical while aiming for strategic goals. It comes down to the personal profile of the individual involved and their experience: This is certainly not a junior role anymore in any way.

It will be a bumpy ride, especially at first, as day-to-day issues will inevitably arise. They will distract and could "nudge you off course", as another of our contributors – a CISO in a large airline organisation – put it, but the challenge is to get back on course and carry on.

Meaningful change will happen over time, through hard work, full commitment to a transformative agenda and maybe bottom-up approaches, but always looking for top-down drivers and leveraging on them when they appear. Once achieved, the long-term rewards – both tangible and reputational – of the transformation delivered will be for the CISO to grab.

#76 The First 100 Days of the New CISO: From Tactical Firefighter to Change Agent (and why it matters to get your hands dirty)

13 September 2018 [Author – Natasha McCabe – with Vincent Viers]

Dealing with the tactical aspects of the function during your first weeks in the job doesn't have to be detrimental to the success of a longer-term transformative agenda

Much has been written about the Chief Information Security Officer and how to best transition into the role for an incoming executive. A somewhat recurring theme to many pieces on the topic revolves around the balance to be found between short-term firefighting and the need to build a strategic elevated vision.

Spending your first weeks in the role dealing with ever-arising tactical issues could indeed steer you away from the longer-term, transformational agenda which is often the reason you're in the job in the first place.

Based on my interviews with several CISO's about their first months in the role, I would like to propose a slightly less dramatic attitude towards tactical firefighting. Turns out that dealing with the day-to-day tactical aspects of the function during your first weeks in the job doesn't have to be detrimental to the success of your longer-term, strategic agenda, and your elevation to the status of change-agent.

In fact, it might be quite the opposite. You should see getting your hands dirty handling day-to-day emergencies as a way towards becoming a successful CISO.

First of all, being able to observe the current reaction and appetite of your organization to tolerate risk and crises will help you tremendously in your assessment work.

Tactical firefighting is arguably the best way to learn about how cybersecurity is actually implemented, pinpoint what doesn't currently work, and help shape your transformation to deliver better outcomes. Pretty much like a real-life fire-safety drill. This can complement – and possibly prove much more informative than – any stakeholder interviews and meetings you will be conducting.

A healthy amount of tactical firefighting will also help you determine the appropriate levels of acceptable and tolerated risk and come up with a more value-added and focused transformation plan – which is what you're looking for, after all. Taking into account how various stakeholders within the organization approach the topic of cybersecurity allows the design of a strategy that's both easier to implement and more efficient.

A particular occurrence of firefighting could serve as a springboard for constructive discussions and some amount of useful storytelling to help design a plan that fits perfectly with the organization's aspirations and needs.

Similarly, this could dramatically help you get your message across to key stakeholders and gather support around your transformation agenda. Indeed, if everything was all rosy and good in the organization, people would likely not put security on top of their priorities. Instead, people will know you, and you in turn will know people. An ambitious transformation plan will also be an easier sell as your usefulness and your reason for being in the role becomes clear to key decisionmakers within the organization.

At least one of my interviewees attributes her lack of success to the fact that she was not able to gather the stakeholder support needed to get the job done, so that's something you should not overlook.

Balancing between tactical firefighting and a strategic agenda remains as important as ever, especially once you realize how the former might help the latter. You will need to win the hearts and mind of your stakeholders, understand the culture of the organization to then be able to drive change and make it stick.

Use it to your advantage to build a security transformation vision that drives value, achieves quick wins, and speaks the business language.

#77 The First 100 Days of the New CISO: Expectations vs. Reality

11 October 2018 [with Vincent Viers]

The situation the new CISO finds on arrival is often different to what they were expecting, but who's to blame?

A painfully recurrent complaint among Chief Information Security Officers (CISO) is the disconnect between what they were promised during the recruitment process, and the actual situation they find upon starting the job.

Indeed, it is quite common to hear freshly-hired CISOs blame their less-than-smooth transition into the role on "broken promises" (some explicit and some simply assumed) such as inadequate resources or insufficient attention dedicated to cybersecurity by key stakeholders.

This is a real issue, as it often results in CISOs not staying long-enough in the job to drive any real or lasting change and leads to the long-term stagnation of the cybersecurity posture of many large firms and of the InfoSec industry at large.

There are several possible reasons for this disconnect between what a new CISO is told, and what they find on arrival:

It might be that the very stakeholders who supported the recruitment of the new CISO into the role are gone by the time the CISO starts. This is not uncommon within large organizations where people – and the priorities they push for ¬– tend to come and go. Little can be done about this – except trying to gather support from new allies within the firm – but it can be very unsettling for the CISO.

Another issue is that hiring managers may not be sufficiently cybersecurity-savvy to frame and express precisely what they are looking for in a CISO. It may result in a misalignment between what the CISO thinks they are in for, and what is actually expected of them. This is often used as an easy excuse by recruiters for an inadequate hire and begs the question of whose fault it actually is.

Beyond those reasonably common issues which could affect any senior position, there are more fundamental problems around cybersecurity senior roles:

Plaguing the whole security industry is the issue of semantics. In cybersecurity, the same term is often used to mean drastically different things – sometimes leading to profound misunderstandings between parties.

Challengingly for the CISO, for example, the concepts of risk or threat can mean different things to different people and quite a lot can end up "lost in translation": For an excessively tech-oriented CISO with little managerial experience, "threats and vulnerabilities" could mean "hackers, ransomware and missing patches" while for their management, it could mean "fraud, insiders and lack of managerial supervision"...

More generally, it could also be that the CISO are part of the problem in that they do not listen enough to key stakeholders to understand what is actually expected of them, often merely focusing on the technology front because it's their comfort zone or their pet subject.

If what's expected of them is to step up as a transversal change-agent, it could become a significant drawback for the CISO and a major source of disappointment for the people they were hired by.

This is the typical type of situation where distrust sets in and the promised resources or budgets do not materialize, leading to more frustration for the CISO.

Conversely, there are still some organizations only looking for a CISO with a highly technical profile to deal with the daily tactical firefighting. In such a context, trying to push for an ambitious cybersecurity transformation plan that the organization is not ready to accept or even understand, could be quite complicated.

An agenda of governance and cultural change could be what the organization needs, but the CISO should not be surprised to be met with reluctance, incomprehension and politics.

They should instead roll up their sleeves and start working relentlessly on convincing, engaging, and finding allies, while addressing tactical quick wins. This is the type of situation where proving your worth by getting your hands dirty could break deadlocks.

Both the CISO and those who hire and manage them must therefore engage in some healthy self-criticism around "broken promises", and most importantly clarify any misunderstanding between them as early as possible.

Leaving after a couple of years – or less – because the CISO doesn't feel empowered or think they've been mis-sold the role does not seem like the right managerial attitude, and the situation has the potential to become self-perpetuating…

Trying to identify and address the underlying misunderstandings and roadblocks would be more beneficial, both to the organization and the individual.

Only then will the CISO be able to feel – and in fact be – successful in the role (and those to come).

#78 Changing Jobs in a Global Pandemic: The New First 100 Days of the CISO

13 May 2021

Focusing ONLY on tactical firefighting is a major mistake, even in a global pandemic

The last twelve month have changed things considerably for the CISO. Cyber security has been centre-stage, and even more now after the SolarWinds and Colonial hacks. Still, this could be a blessing or a curse.

The pandemic keeps evolving on a global scale, and while some countries may be reaching the end of the tunnel, others are still in the midst of the most dramatic phases.

Global business is still significantly impacted, and there is no sign of a "new normal" in sight for many industries.

Still, people are changing jobs, and CISOs in particular, as many firms wake up to the need to ramp up cyber security measures in the face of the accelerated digitization of their business or their large-scale move to remote working.

But, in the face of the new situation created by the pandemic, the approach we highlighted back in 2018 around the "First 100 Days of the CISO" needs adjusting.

It still makes sense for any incoming executive to approach their first period in a new job in a structured way, to meet with business stakeholders and listen to their expectations first in relation to the role, then to build a strategic framework addressing those, and then an execution framework to deliver it.

But two aspects have changed fundamentally:

While stakeholders are more likely to recognise cyber security as an important agenda item, they are still likely to be focused on short-term objectives, either in terms of crisis response or in terms of bounce-back strategy. They may not be receptive to long-term views; as a matter of fact, they may not have any form of long-term visibility for the moment, as the global pandemic continues to unfold world-wide.

That's the second main issue: 100 days is probably an irrelevant timeframe here, irrespective of how you frame it (back in 2018, we articulated it into 6 days, 6 weeks and 6 months encompassing around 100 business days). Nobody can be sure how the world will be like in 100 days, let alone in 6 months.

So how should an incoming CISO approach their new role?

Meeting with key stakeholders and team members as soon as realistically possible, and listening to their objectives, concerns and priorities, is still key as a starting point.

Back in 2018, we strongly advocated in favour of travelling and meeting face to face – where required – to develop a stronger personal bond: This is not likely to be possible for the short-term, so most of those discussions will have to take place remotely. Let's face it: This is a problem, and the absence of direct personal interaction could distort the perception the new CISO develops of the firm and its culture – for good or for bad. The most important for the CISO at this stage is to remain aware of that. But establishing direct communication channels with the business – as solid as they can be at the moment – is more essential than ever.

Second, it is likely – as we have already highlighted – that a short-termist agenda will emerge from those discussions. The temptation will be extremely high for the CISO to focus only on alleged low-hanging fruits and on firefighting, at least until the worst of the crisis is over. To be honest, this is the way many CISOs have traditionally approached their first 100 days anyway, so more than a "temptation", it will be a line of least resistance – or even a well-trodden path – for some.

As a matter of fact, we highlighted back in 2018 that it was a dangerous path to follow and a "curse", unlikely to lead to the development of truly transformational dynamics around cyber security: That is still the case, but, realistically, it will be a trend difficult to oppose for the new CISO.

In fact, this is the very element that makes the new first 100 days of the CISO far more complex than ever before.

It is no longer just a matter of balancing tactical and strategic objectives while validating strategy and execution frameworks; it could be about doing this in absence of clear strategic visibility from the business, as the path out of the COVID crisis emerges, and in a context where those directions may evolve or change, depending on the turns the crisis may still take.

The new CISO must talk constantly with business stakeholders, to understand how this context is moving, and build their own cyber security strategic options – possibly scenario-based, and ready to be embedded into the post-crisis business strategy as it aggregates. And all this in parallel to short-term tactical work to keep the lights on.

Make no mistakes: This is now becoming a matter of survival for the CISO role at any form of senior leadership level.

"Constant firefighting downgrades the role and the CISO must fight to avoid its gravitational pull" we wrote back in 2018.

Focus ONLY on low hanging fruits and alleged quick wins, fail to leverage on the opportunities presented by the pandemic to cement cyber security as a true dimension of business strategy, and the new CISO could find their role relegated forever to middle-management layers, alongside other technical operational matters.

COVID-19,
Cyber Security
and the
"New Normal"

#79 Can you still Afford "not to afford" Cyber Security?

6 February / 15 May 2020

COVID-19 changes the game: Now is not the time to risk a cyber-attack.

Earlier ransomware incidents that have affected organisations such Travelex in the UK or Bouygues in France profoundly question the way cyber security has been managed – historically – in many large firms. And they add their names to an ever growing "hall of shame" which already includes British Airways, Marriott, Equifax and – sadly – countless others.

Large firms with multi-million IT and security budgets should not end up in that mess. Period.

Calling in one of the Big 4 firms to "sort things out" afterwards will not cut it anymore. At the heart of the matter, is not just the need to "do things" (protective and layered "defence-in-depth" measures are well known and have been for decades) but the governance surrounding execution in those firms, the way the prioritisation of security investment was handled over the years, and the cultural and managerial aspects surrounding those.

"We can't afford this" is an excuse we have been hearing too often with senior executives around security over the years. Many CISOs take it as budgetary constraints. It is simply adverse prioritisation. And if security is not visibly towards the top of the agenda with management, you cannot expect good execution to follow regardless of the investments you make.

One trait many of the firms affected recently by cyber security incidents had in common (pre COVID-19), was their relatively good economic health. Those were not failing businesses chronically losing money or drastically challenged by digital disruption, as could have been the case for example in the retail sector. They were healthy and established market players churning up healthy profits.

How did they use to assess the threats they face? How did they manage their levels of exposure or protection against those? How did they determine the investments necessary to ensure adequate protection?

Clearly, not very well…

One thing is certain: They were not really short of cash – at the time. It may be a simplistic view from a CFO perspective, but the reality is that – post breach – money invariably used to appear out of nowhere to get things "fixed".

That's the most pathetic part of all those incidents: Shameless executives, who previously would have argued that they "could not afford" security measures, handing out millions in search of non-existent quick-wins or technical silver-bullets. And shameless tech vendors and security "consultants" lining up, without for a second daring to tell their clients what they need to hear: Buying more tech won't help you, until you address the cultural and governance attitudes which have led you in that mess in the first place: Endemic short-termism, cognitive biases, or frankly in some cases, threat ignorance and lip service to compliance requirements.

Of course, once the entire business has been down for several days, priorities are put into perspective and mindsets change, but for how long?

Across the street, various competitors or suppliers would have been rattled and may also start thinking differently, but again, for how long?

Once the dust has settled, losses are just losses; they may not please the shareholders, but in a context where many things could go wrong for large firms, do they really matter if the health of the business is strong? For St Gobain, Maersk and others – badly hit by the 2017 NotPetya outbreak – lost sales associated with the cyber-attack were estimated in the hundreds of millions and direct costs related to crisis in the tens of millions. Unpleasant, not invisible but manageable – in good times – on an otherwise healthy multi-billion balance sheet.

Frankly, those days have gone. The COVID-19 crisis changes the landscape totally around cyber-attacks, and that type of cynical approach now borders on plain negligence.

Which business can now afford "not-to-afford" good cyber security measures, in a context where most remaining activity has shifted online, and we are all dependent on digital services?

Security has become essential to keeping the lights on, and nobody can risk a cyber attack in the middle of all this. At the same time, cash has become precious and the business outlook is unclear.

But prioritising against security spending seems unreasonable, even in the face of massive cost reductions, and in particular in organisations where current cyber maturity levels are low.

Now is the time to look at those maturity problems in the face and to focus the scarce resources available where they will have most impact. But cutting security spending to the ground in the midst of the COVID-19 crisis would be disastrous.

#80 Is the Coronavirus killing the GDPR?

16 April 2020

In practice, the COVID-19 crisis has put regulatory powers on hold but as things stand, two forces seem to be at play.

It has been clear from the start that the role of the privacy regulators – and their attitude towards enforcement – would be key to the acceptance and embedding of the new data privacy practices embodied in the GDPR.

Right now, in practical terms, the privacy regulators cannot act beyond providing advice and support. Enforcing punitive action in the context of the COVID-19 economic meltdown would be at best insensitive – at worst, it would damage their credibility irremediably.

Further, their approach to enforcement since May 2018 – as summarised in the latest report from DLA Piper released in February – shows that they have been targeting mostly small to mid-size firms with small to mid-size fines (for small to mid-size infringements); this is probably not sustainable as this segment of the economic fabric is most at risk from the Coronavirus crisis.

And the two large fines – proposed by the UK ICO for the British Airways and Marriott data breaches – are still undergoing some form of legal challenge (for what is in the public domain on the matter).

Again, it would be highly controversial for the regulators or the courts to uphold those fines: What is the point of fining British Airways £183M, in a context where they are going to require billions in state aid to survive?

So more than ever, the privacy regulators have a delicate game to play. And behind all that, and the approach they will decide to take, lurks the shadow of their real independence from politicians. And a key question around the duration during which the exceptional COVID-19 situation could justify a relaxation of the regulatory grip.

Public interest for data privacy matters is heightened by remote working and lockdown conditions.

In parallel, as the lockdown makes society entirely dependent on digital services, segments of the public and of the media are waking up to a few realities around data and privacy.

The outcry coming from some corners around the videoconference platform Zoom is laughable in most respects.

"If you're not paying for the product, you are the product" has been the mantra behind countless of those internet platforms for the best part of the last two decades. In other words, your personal data is often the real currency on the internet instead of your hard-earned cash.

Their terms were obscure and one-sided, and they were sending data to Facebook … big deal … show me one app which doesn't …

Oh… and if you don't password-protect your conference and place a link on a public website, some uninvited people may join you…

And if you use an old version of (any) software, it may contain vulnerabilities that hackers can exploit…

Frankly, none of this is new, except the amount of interest and the public reaction.

More interesting is the debate around the use of mobile phones geolocation data in the fight against the Coronavirus.

The use of (properly) anonymised data in the exceptional context of the COVID-19 crisis to measure the general effectiveness of the lockdown (i.e. whether people are following it well or not – collectively) does not seem to infringe on the provisions of the GDPR (as long as the data is properly kept, no longer than is necessary to serve the purpose etc…); there is almost some form of "legitimate interest" behind that many GDPR practitioners will be familiar with.

The use of geolocation data in the context of a large scale testing programme is more problematic: There may be a legitimate interest in using an app – with consent – to monitor the movements of symptomatic or asymptomatic virus carriers, and retrospectively for contact tracing. Whether it is legitimate to extend that to healthy or immune people is another matter. Together with the way the data will be used to enforce any form of lockdown and not just monitor it, and the precedent it may create.

Overall, it seems clear at this stage that those options might have a role to play in any exit or post-COVID-19 strategy, but they will have to be handled with care by politicians and regulators at a time of heightened public emotions around those matters.

Like everything else, our perception around data and privacy will be very different when we re-emerge at the end of the COVID-19 crisis.

The privacy regulators will have to adjust their game and the GDPR may have to evolve. But the public debate shows that the interest on those matters is high, and that's likely to stay.

#81 COVID-19, Cyber Security and the "New Normal"

30 April 2020

It is hard not to see tech, security and privacy coming out stronger.

As we all struggle with lockdown conditions and the impact the COVID-19 crisis is having on our lives and our businesses, one sentiment seems to prevail: The sense that – somehow – life after the coronavirus will not return exactly to "what it used to be".

Discussions and commentaries abound on what that "new normal" will be like, but they all bump across the same hurdle: The time horizon towards which they are looking cannot really be defined right now.

Frankly, at the minute, the only certainty is still uncertainty, and there are just too many scenarios and too much unknown to plan ahead properly, unless you are prepared to consider a seriously multi-threaded strategy: Will lockdown exit scenarios be successful? Will there be further outbreaks and how will governments react? When will free movement of people resume? Locally? Nationally? Internationally? How long does natural immunity actually last and when will a vaccine be ready or deployed? As they stand, will governments rescue plans be sufficient? How many businesses will go bankrupt regardless? Etc…

Nobody can really see beyond the few weeks ahead, and that paralyses – rightly – any mid- to long-term decision making in most businesses. In addition, most have had to take drastic cash conservation measures, with – amongst other measures – many top executives agreeing to major pay cuts, while numbers of staff go on paid or unpaid leave. Money is scarce for many and could be for a long time.

But from a technology and cyber security perspective, there are three lessons already emerging:

Remote working works

First, from a technology perspective, the large scale remote working experiment we are having to endure is simply working: Platforms have scaled, and networks have not collapsed. We may or may not like it, but we are starting to adjust to new ways of interacting. More generally, the digital economy has successfully scaled up at pace and the COVID-19 crisis has dramatically accelerated the digital transformation of many sectors. It is impossible to say what the long-term impact will be (e.g. to what extend will we continue to work from home), but this is bound to bring a positive outlook for the tech industry at large.

Cyber security is critical

Second, over the last six weeks and in the face of countless scams and fraud attempts, we have had in front of us the largest real-life cyber security awareness campaign anyone could ever have imagined, and this is bound to have a significant cultural impact on people, in particular if the lockdown continues or comes back. Cyber security has had to be on the agenda, as a necessary dimension of lives and business activities now entirely dependent on digital services. Nobody can risk a cyber-attack right now, and good cyber security measures have become key to keeping the lights on. One cannot imagine cyber security moving down the priority list with senior executives post-COVID.

Privacy concerns are being re-enforced

Finally, privacy has not gone off the radar. If anything, the debate around digital contact tracing and the use of mobile apps has re-ignited the public interest around personal data and state surveillance. One can argue about the timeliness of all that and the need for exceptional measures during exceptional times, but it remains a sign of healthy democracies that it's taking place. Where it will leave pre-existing regulations such as GDPR or CCPA – and how it will impact the long-term role and credibility of privacy regulators – remains open for debate, but that's another matter.

Nobody really knows what the "new normal" will be like and when – and how – the dust will settle. But it is hard not to see tech, security and privacy coming out stronger.

#82 Cyber Security: Beyond a Mere Operational Approach

11 June 2020

The post-COVID winners will be those who treat it strategically now

C-level executives must stop looking at cyber security as a mere operational matter: Something which is below them and is dealt with somewhere below them in the organisation. It is the type of mental attitude which is has led to twenty years of maturity stagnation in real terms across the security industry, in spite of the billions spent with tech vendors.

Talking about industry stagnation is a way of highlighting that the security industry keeps going round in circles and that topics – such as the timely deployment of security patches for example – keep coming back regularly towards the top of the agenda, although they have been known – and could have been addressed – for more than a decade.

But as a matter of fact, the situation is getting worse, and firms – large and small – have been facing a non-stop tidal wave of cyber attacks over the past few years in spite of the proliferation of tech products in that space.

Fundamentally, pure operational approaches to cyber security have failed. They have not managed to keep in phase with the digital transformation of many businesses, the emergence of cloud solutions and the de-perimeterization of the enterprise. They have fallen victim to adverse prioritization and internal politics in many large firms or have not been able to focus beyond illusory quick wins.

In fact, taking a pure operational approach to cyber security fails because it downgrades a complex matter and negates its true dimension. It is not – and has never been – a purely technical problem. The protection of the enterprise – by its employees – against external threats is rooted in corporate values and management practices. And that's where the solution should start.

Good and clear governance must be in place around cyber security and be visible up to the top. This must now be a Board matter in the face of non-stop cyber-attacks, and it must be visibly owned by a Board member.

It is also a transversal problem, and not just a technical one. Business units and support functions must be directly involved in any cyber security programme of work, not just IT.

There will be no magical or instant solution where cyber security maturity levels are low. Improvement will require transformative work at a number of levels across the enterprise and probably over the mid to long-term.

The current situation around COVID-19 makes the message ever harder to accept, as uncertainty dominates, budgets tighten and priorities have to be set ruthlessly. But the hard realities around cyber security remain the same. And buying some tech silver bullet is not likely to solve it for you, in spite of what countless vendors would like you to believe.

At the same time, maintaining good cyber security has never been more essential, as the digital transformation accelerates and the economy at large shifts towards operating models which present much broader attack surfaces to cyber threats and are – effectively – entirely dependent on secure and stable practices.

Post-COVID, concerns will return of regulatory and legal friction around the security of personal data, and the corporate resilience to cyber-attacks. Privacy concerns have not disappeared during the lockdown. In fact, the debate around the introduction of tracing apps in some western countries has highlighted the vitality of the topic and it is likely – going forward – that citizens and customers will demand a greater sense of purpose from businesses and greater respect for their personal data.

Good cyber security – and data privacy – practices are essential pillars supporting digital trust, and digital trust will be the cornerstone of the post-COVID "new normal".

Now is the time to treat cyber security strategically – not tactically – and to embed it into your culture – not just your technology or your operations.

The post-COVID winners will be those who seize the moment.

#83 Post-COVID Outlook for Cyber Security: New Normal ... Looking a Lot like the Old

16 July 2020

The COVID crisis has not changed the cyber security fundamentals: What will the new normal be like?

Two recent reports highlight the current cyber security paradox: While the COVID pandemic has turned business and society upside down, well-established cyber security practices – some known for decades – remain the best way to protect yourself.

It might not be the message the authors of those reports wanted to convey, but it remains the dominant impression.

The first one, from the World Economic Forum, published in May ("Cybersecurity Leadership Principles: Lessons learnt during the COVID-19 pandemic to prepare for the new normal" – WEF – 26 May 2020[1]) is once again a superlative summary of good practices, which in the end hardly moves the needle. We commented along the same lines on one of their earlier reports last year.

Using buzzwords like "resilience" instead of "security" or "continuity" does not disguise the fact that 80% or more of the "lessons learnt" highlighted in the report (e.g. "focus on critical services", "implement meaningful metrics" or "practice crisis management plans") can be summarised in three words: Follow Good Practice… More than ever, doing the right thing around cyber security, seems to consist of doing now what you should have done ten years ago…

Obviously, if those are still valuable "lessons learnt" worth highlighting to world leaders, it implies they were not properly in place pre-COVID in spite of having been known as security good practices for decades, but the report stays well clear from discussing why…

1 https://www.weforum.org/reports/cybersecurity-leadership-principles-lessons-learnt-during-the-covid-19-pandemic-to-prepare-for-the-new-normal

The second report, from InfoSecurity Magazine, published in June ("State of Cybersecurity Report 2020" – InfoSecurity Magazine – 3 June 2020[1]) offers – as expected – a more technical perspective but points in the same direction with regards to its key takeaways.

The key importance of human elements in cyber security or the fact that "the evolution of the cloud is driving innovation whilst also exposing organizations to new security and privacy challenges" are nothing new.

It is evident that the COVID pandemic has accented and accelerated those, but once again, the cloud was not born out of COVID and good practices in those areas should have been in place for decades.

As a matter of fact, our 2019 report on the "Language of Security[2]" (built on the semantics analysis of the content of 17 annual "Global Information Security Surveys" from leading firm EY, spanning the period 2002-2018) shows without ambiguity cloud security considerations dominating the period 2010-2011-2012 before receding dramatically.

The shift of focus away from compliance is also something our 2019 report highlighted, but again this is a ten years old long-term trend starting around 2010 (and arguably one of the key findings of our research): The first decade of this century was the true "compliance" decade for cyber security; the last decade has been a "realisation" decade dominated by incidents and threats considerations, leading to the acceptance by many business leaders of a "when-not-if" paradigm around cyber-attacks.

The "when-not-if" paradigm creates completely new challenges for CISOs and CIOs: Old and well-established security basics still go a long way to ensure protection but the challenges are now firmly around execution, while roadblocks remain rooted in governance dysfunctions and short-termist business cultures.

The COVID crisis does not change any of that but it does aggravate short-termist business tendencies and will constrain budgetary resources dramatically in most industries.

---

1 https://www.infosecurity-magazine.com/white-papers/state-of-cybersecurity-report-2020/

2 https://securitytransformation.com/wp-content/uploads/2017/07/CyberSecurity-A-Look-Across-2-Decades-FINAL1-19SEP2019.pdf

If one thing is going to change (for some tech vendors at least), is that throwing money indiscriminately at the cyber security problems in the hope of making them disappear is going to stop: Spending and resources will have to be focused where they can have the most impact and that has to start with a sound appreciation of critical assets and their risk posture. But again, focusing on those "crown jewels" should be seen as one of the oldest and best-established good practices…

It looks like the "new normal" is definitely going to look a lot like the old.

#84 Budgeting for Cyber Security post-COVID: Three Golden Rules for the C-Suite[1]

3 September 2020

This is not just about tech, and there is no tech silver bullet which can buy you cyber resilience

The COVID crisis is presenting most businesses with unprecedented situations – for good, bad or worse. Uncertainty still dominates but the recession ahead is likely to be deep and could be protracted. Millions of people have already lost their jobs across the world, and many organisations are bracing for further significant spending cuts, in the face of a dwindling economic activity. Even in thriving sectors, budgetary caution seems to be the norm amongst C-level executives.

One thing the pandemic has not pushed off the radar, is cyber security. As a matter of fact, the volume of cyber-attacks increased to "alarming levels" according to Interpol during the heart of the crisis. For businesses now totally dependent on remote working, e-commerce or digital supply chains, a serious security breach is the last thing they want…

CEOs, CFOs and CIOs should not jump to ready-made conclusions around cyber security ahead of their next budgeting round. Here are three golden rules for them to consider as they plan ahead.

Think carefully before making drastic arbitrary cuts around cyber security

Consider carefully and without complacency your actual level of cyber security maturity, and the level of digital dependency the COVID crisis has brought upon you.

Look at the bigger picture: Only serious defence-in-depth can guarantee you a degree of cyber resilience. That means the actual

---

1 You can watch JC Gaillard talk through the content of this article at the DigitalLeaders Week on 14th October 2020 on the Corix Partners YouTube channel > https://www.youtube.com/watch?v=dyzOJgdEVOw

application of protective measures at preventative, detective, mitigative and reactive levels. Doing pen tests every now and then and sending awareness emails to the staff twice a year – while probably better than not doing anything at all – does not constitute a security practice.

Do not ignore your degree of dependency on third-party business partners or cloud service providers, and the implied degree of trust you are placing on the solidity of THEIR cyber defences. How much do you really know of what they are actually doing to protect your data or your processes?

If you don't think you are in a good place on those matters, now is not the time to cut cyber security spending to the ground.

Focus budgeting on the protection of key assets

Equally, now is not the time to try to solve all the problems you may have around cyber security: You need to identify your key assets and focus efforts on those, whatever they might be: Systems, business processes, business units or geographies.

Focus on clear, simple, tangible, affordable and measurable tasks with a short to mid-term horizon. Now is not the time to engage in multi-year projects, which the general economic uncertainty is likely to affect or kill.

Focus budgeting on areas where you know you can execute

Finally, now is not the time for large-scale and complex pet-projects: Ignore the sirens from the tech industry – there are countless vendors out there with their own "silver bullet" to solve all your problems – and focus on areas where you have the skills to deliver and know you can execute: It's only the actual implementation of protective measures, across the real breadth and depth of the enterprise, which will protect your business. Not snake oil and false promises.

And limit the complexity of what you are trying to achieve to a level your teams can manage and absorb. Consider carefully the dependencies between the security tasks you are undertaking and the cross-silos implications amongst stakeholders: You may need the involvement of HR, legal, procurement or business executives depending on what you are trying to achieve (for example around identity management, or data privacy compliance). Make sure the priorities are clear for them too.

Fundamentally, remember: This is not just about tech, and there is no tech silver bullet which can buy you cyber resilience – irrespective of what countless vendors would like you to believe. It can only come through concerted action at people, process and technology levels, and the real execution of protective measures.

#85 Remote Work, Leadership and Cyber Security

7 January 2021

Transformational opportunity for firms, or tactical trap for the CISO?

As the COVID crisis continues to develop, one thing is becoming clearer and clearer: Remote working is here to stay, in some form or another; probably as hybrid work. Technically, it has scaled, and it has worked. Throughout the pandemic, it has enabled many industries worldwide to continue operating, and many people to keep their jobs.

From an acceptance perspective, it's another story. I am yet to meet a single person who would endorse it fully. At one extreme, it disturbs family life, increases isolation, and can lead to depression or burnout. More generally, people accept that it can bring valuable flexibility – in exchange of necessary adjustments in their work-life routines – but most miss the camaraderie of the office, the coffee machine discussions and the afterwork bonding.

I have heard many people around me say they were working considerably more under lockdown than before; whether your productivity actually increases through back-to-back conference calls is another matter, but that was their perception.

From a leadership perspective, it's also another story. The shift to remote work has been extremely fast at the start of national lockdowns. Throughout 2020, most of the organisations which adopted it, kept it as their main operating mode throughout the year; very few have "returned to the office" at scale.

But leading through remote interactions has little to do with leading through direct human interactions.

It requires a different form of empathy, and more importantly, it requires an adjustment in the attitude of the leader, in absence of all the subjective context provided by informal interactions and body language. Face to face, a good manager should sense if the person on the other side of the table is comfortable, uncomfortable, or nervous; in a meeting room, there are always some people more engaged than others across the table, from those jumping up and down to those falling asleep; over a conference call, most of those signals – which a leader should otherwise capture and address – are often lost…

Very few leaders have been trained in any way for this; there was no time for it at the start of the crisis – or since. Some would have had natural leadership qualities and would have adjusted, but many have struggled and are still struggling.

As the COVID crisis unravels and people adjust to some form of new normal, we could be heading for a multi-year period of remote or hybrid work in many industries, with an unprepared middle and upper-middle management layer, struggling and overworked, and not learning – through human interaction – the unvaluable leadership skills they will need at the next stage in their careers. There is potentially a concerning "lost generation" problem here if things persist.

Why is this particularly relevant for cyber security? Because the role of the CISO is already in transition, and its complexity makes it particularly vulnerable to that type of situation.

If they want to avoid the firefighting trap, CISOs have to lead by influence, working across silos, with business units, support functions and the Board, not only to drive the right security culture, but also to embed the right security processes and tools across the business.

More and more, because of the transversal complexity of cybersecurity matters in the modern enterprise, it is the management acumen, the political intelligence, the personal gravitas that make a successful CISO, more than their raw technical knowledge.

Building those relationships and driving those interactions face to face is hard enough, particularly in large or global organisations. But doing it remotely is close to impossible, in particular to the unprepared CISO, or in industries where management has been incapable of looking beyond the mere tactical day-to-day throughout the COVID crisis (instead of looking for transformative opportunities).

Although it has brought cyber security under the spotlight and might bring more resources in some industries (where digital is key to keeping the lights on), the COVID crisis might become the ultimate "tactical trap" for the CISO, preventing them from developing beyond day-to-day firefighting and extending the spectre of the "lost decade" we diagnosed in earlier work in 2019.

Change can only come from the top, with senior management embedding cyber security in strategic objectives as a pillar to the stability of their new operating models, moving away from mere operational approaches, and creating a new governance bond across all cyber security stakeholders.

It will probably require new organisational models. This is something we have been advocating since 2018 which we will continue to explore here and with techuk.

#86 Cyber Security can be a Pillar of any Corporate "Build Back Better" Agenda

3 June 2021

But are the CISOs ready for it?

A comment left on one of my articles made me think: How can cyber security leaders drive a long-term transformative agenda, with a business and a board that cannot see beyond the short-term?

I see several angles worth discussing around the way the question was put, which may help break some deadlocks.

Endemic short-termism is a management problem which has been plaguing large organisations for decades. There are industries where it makes sense because they are rooted in short-term cycles; there are industries where it doesn't and simply reflects an obsessive focus on shareholders return.

Two trends are worth bearing in mind in the particular times we are going through:

First of all, the COVID crisis has obliterated – for now – any type of long-term perspective across many industries; you cannot blame your business for thinking short-term, where – frankly – there is no other option.

At the same time, corporate "Build Back Better" agendas are driving a focus on purpose, ESG matters and a move towards stakeholder capitalism, away from shareholder capitalism; success on those fronts will require vision and long-term leadership: We will not "build back better" in that way overnight…

So, understanding why their business is focusing only on short-term matters, has to be a starting point for cyber security leaders looking to position longer-term objectives, as well as understanding where the business and the Board are around the "Build Back Better" pivot, because that may drive a change in focus.

Ideally, you would use that pivot to embed cyber security and privacy as pillars in the firm's "Build Back Better" objectives, but to achieve that, cyber security leaders need to have access to the board agenda and this is not something they can dictate; this is something you build up over time through management and political acumen, and also through the trust deposited in you, which would have come from your execution capabilities.

CISOs simply pushing bottom-up technical narratives and metrics towards the board often fail at building up that type of relationship. They downgrade their function and themselves by limiting its scope to a technical and operational dimension, and the board ends up seeing them as mere "firefighters".

The COVID crisis would have accentuated that tendency in many organisations: CISOs who only bring short-term technical problems to the board, will only hear short-term answers in return, and over time, simply become incapable of breaking into a longer-term agenda, because they have not built up that credibility when they could have done.

Of course, there must be organisations where the board does not want to hear anything else around cyber security, because they feel this is simply an operational matter which lives a long way below them. For those, it is often enough to have the CISO wheeled-in once or twice a year, before swiftly moving on to more "important" matters. Unfortunately, cyber attacks have been relentless, their impact – financial and reputational – has sky-rocketed and that type of attitude is increasingly becoming more and more difficult to sustain.

Still, to break into the long-term agenda with the board, cyber security leaders need the right levers.

Since 2019, we have been advocating that anchoring cyber security and privacy as pillars of a firms' ESG strategy could be a good start: There is no doubt that corporate "Build Back Better" agendas are likely to help with that in most organisations, but only for cyber security leaders who have managed to build the right channels to tap into it.

For the others, unfortunately, short-term firefighting, accentuated by the pandemic could become a trap difficult to escape.

Conclusion

#87 Cyber Security: Who Cares? and What Happens Next?

11 August 2016 [with Vincent Viers]

In recent years, the topic of digital transformation has moved to the top of the agenda in the business world. However, most of these discussions all too often seem to bypass the issue of cyber security. This is hard to understand in a context where many studies have clearly illustrated that cyber and privacy threats have started to damage the trust of consumers and have the potential to destroy considerable amounts of value.

If sound cyber security practices and respect for customers' personal data are key pillars to any successful and lasting digital transformation, why are these topics of so little interest to senior executives?

There are two sides to this deep-rooted problem

And both the business world and the technology world are responsible in their own ways for avoiding the real issues.

On the business side, it's quite simple: Corporate logics are dominated by considerations of short-term maximisation – be it for profit or shareholder value. Security does not generate revenues therefore it does not figure in this equation. The absence of security measures may eventually harm the trust of customers but this is seen as a long-term problem. As a result, many organisations approach cyber security from a reactive, tick-in-the-box point of view and it remains a back room topic that does not seem to provide tangible value in the short-run. As a matter of fact, in an efficient cyber security world, nothing happens. And for many business leaders, should something happen in that space, it will just be another problem for somebody to fix – in a context where many things can go wrong every day in large corporations.

But simply dealing with the complex and constantly evolving issues associated with cyber security in an ad-hoc manner without placing them in their context and resolving root causes cannot bring change.

This is the typical area where the mere quest for immediate solutions simply leads to long-term stagnation, as surveys keep highlighting year after year.

This is part of a broader business problem and this short-sighted mindset, as we have come to realise in recent years, can prove to be damaging to the long-term viability of many organisations.

This short-termist doxa reigns over every business schools, MBA programs and consulting groups where many executives are formed. After all, "in the long run we are all dead" wrote Keynes. Senior executives are taught to generate revenue and to focus on their bottom-lines; not to manage hypothetical loss-avoidance. And when they are taught to manage risk, they tend to focus on the actuarial frequency of risk events more than on probability which is always considerably more complex and costly to estimate.

In the cyber security world, where actuarial data is just not available (or trustworthy) and threats evolve constantly, this mental scheme creates the background for the wrong decisions to be made.

Cyber threats have historically been perceived as low-frequency events with low – or at least manageable – associated impacts.

Day after day, events in the news demonstrate that this is no longer the case

However, the message is only filtering through very slowly and clearly other forces are at play that are still preventing large organisations from pre-emptively transitioning towards an effective and pro-active InfoSec strategy.

Nobel prize laureate Daniel Kahneman has shown that the subjective evaluation of the probability of an event happening depends partially on how easily the occurrence of this event can be imagined. This bias of imaginability might help explain why so few key executives – puzzled by the technical complexity of the issue and the fact that it seems to be constantly evolving – realise that cyber-attacks are not a matter of if anymore, but a matter of when. The true lack of understanding of the issue by many executives also spurs a paralysing fear of pushing much-needed InfoSec reforms forward.

At best, many organisations tend to reassure themselves by pouring money into ineffective technical solutions they do not quite understand either but that somehow "put ticks in boxes", address artificially audit or compliance concerns, and make them feel like they have dealt with the problem and that they can now focus on revenue-generating business operations.

Issues, however, do not disappear simply because we stop thinking about them

Should any cyber security incident or near-miss happen (or receive wide-spread media coverage such as the TalkTalk incident in the UK in 2015), of course knee-jerk reactions and instant responses will be demanded, but those attitudes simply perpetuate the short-termist agenda and quite often create more problems than they solve.

If the Business world is not asking for it, the Technology world is very unlikely to draw the attention of top-executives towards the real nature of their cyber security problems. Eagerly leveraging their clients' lack of real understanding, many tech firms – equally blinded by short-termist considerations – have been very happy to look elsewhere or sell them highly technical point solutions without addressing underlying governance, people and process issues. Of course, over the mid to long-term, those approaches rarely deliver the necessary levels of change around cyber security, and the whole topic ends up being perceived as negative, complex, costly and boring.

There are only two ways this destructive spiral will be broken

In the long-run, market dynamics and the digital transformation of society and business models may be enough to make businesses care about cyber security, as consumers become increasingly concerned not only about functionality of products but also about their safety, and the usage and protection of their personal data. If and when cyber security becomes a revenue generating competitive advantage, the lines will start shifting for good.

Meanwhile, if consumers' perception around cyber security and privacy moves faster than businesses and technology can – or are willing to – adjust, politicians and bureaucrats will step in and react by imposing or tightening regulation. In many ways, this is already happening in Europe around data privacy.

In all cases, those businesses that have taken cyber security and privacy seriously from the start are likely to be ahead and to stay ahead in the digital transformation game.

Appendix –
Cyber Security:
A Look Across
Two Decades

#88 Cyber Security: A Look Across Two Decades

7 November 2019

The Security industry talks a lot about what could go wrong … but not so much about how to improve things

Research released by The Security Transformation Research Foundation, ahead of the Cyber Security Leadership Summit in Berlin on 12-14 November 2019, highlights significant trends in the way the language of security has evolved across the last 2 decades.

The foundation analysed the semantics content of 17 annual "Global Information Security Surveys" from leading firm EY, spanning the period 2002-2018.

By looking at the frequency of keyword markers and how those frequencies have evolved over time, the research puts in evidence a clear demarcation between 2 periods.

While across the period up to 2009, the language is clearly dominated by considerations around risk and compliance, those considerations clearly subside during the following decade and are replaced by concerns around threats and incidents.

A language bias analysis also highlights that while the language during the first decade had a clear positive and managerial bias, again the trend changes across the last decade and the language becomes considerably more negative and more technical.

Concerns around the Cloud make a sharp outburst at the junction of the 2 decades and dominate considerations in 2010, 2011 and 2012 then seem to vanish into normality and acceptance.

A sense of realisation seems to dominate the junction between the 2 decades: The realisation that this is no longer JUST about Compliance and Risk, that Tech is changing, threats are real and incidents do impact Business.

The business language in the surveys also sharpens throughout the period, but considerations around execution, people, culture and skills clearly dwindle.

Overall, as the foundation puts it, "the Security industry tends to talk a lot about what could go wrong … but not as much about could be done to fix things", with keyword markers such as risk, threat, compliance or incident 3.5 times more frequent across all surveys than governance, budget, delivery, priority, culture or skill.

As we look towards the next decade, the industry must pivot towards a clearer execution focus: Security cannot be seen any more JUST as a matter of risk appetite or as a box-checking exercise; equally, constant firefighting is no longer sufficient as the "when not if" paradigm takes root in the boardroom and senior executives demand real results, often in exchange of very significant investments.

Security must become a delivery imperative, and where existing maturity levels are low, the CISO must become a true transformational leader.

Cyber Security: A Look Across Two Decades

Results from the quantitative analysis of the semantics content of 17 annual **Global Information Security Surveys** from EY spanning the period 2002-2019

2010_EY_GISS
2009_EY_GISS
2008_EY_GISS
2007_EY_GISS
2006_EY_GISS
2005_EY_GISS
2004_EY_GISS
2003_EY_GISS
2002_EY_GISS

2018-2019_EY_GISS
2017-2018_EY_GISS
2016-2017_EY_GISS
2015_EY_GISS
2014_EY_GISS
2013_EY_GISS
2012_EY_GISS
2011_EY_GISS

Cyber Security: A Look Across Two Decades

We performed a quantitative analysis of the frequency of keyword markers across a set of 77,750 meaningful words extracted from the text of the 17 GISS reports

5 key findings, as indicators on how we (Security Practitioners) communicate with senior stakeholders and how our language has evolved over the past 2 decades

Why Did We Do This?

To build a quantitative understanding on how the focus and priorities of the Security industry have evolved throughout the last 2 decades

Why did we analyse semantics instead of results?

No access to underlying data sets meant we could not compare or normalise results in a meaningful way

Semantics reveal the way the results were interpreted and the language used in such analysis is a good indicator of the industry focus points year after year

Why the EY GISS?

- The timespan covered
  It was actually first produced in 1998 but we could not trace the first 4 issues
- The consistency in layout, size and approach
- The level of depth and general quality of the analysis

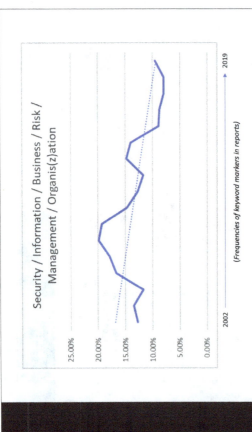

Security / Information / Business / Risk / Management / Organis(z)ation

25.00%

20.00%

15.00%

10.00%

5.00%

0.00%

2002

2019

(Frequencies of keyword markers in reports)

We tend to talk about Security in more and more specific terms

Cyber Security: A Look Across Two Decades

Finding 1

- The most common words are generic

- But while the language in the reports is dominated by generic terms, their overall proportion tends to be diminishing

Cyber Security: A Look Across Two Decades

Finding 2

When adding a sentiment analysis layer over the data, the 2 decades appear to be split by a clear semantic shift towards a more <u>technical and more negative language</u>

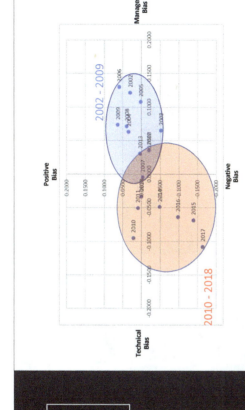

If our language around Security has become more specific, it has also become more technical and more negative

Cyber Security: A Look Across Two Decades

Finding 3

This split reflects a significant shift in focus across the 2 decades

The Compliance and Risk considerations which dominate the period 2002-2009 are clearly replaced by Incidents and Threats considerations during the following decade

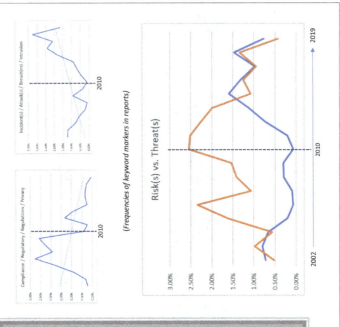

(Frequencies of keyword markers in reports)

Risk(s) vs. Threat(s)

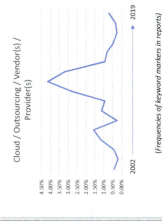

Cloud / Outsourcing / Vendor(s) / Provider(s)

(Frequencies of keyword markers in reports)

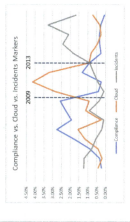

Compliance vs. Cloud vs. Incidents Markers

— Compliance — Cloud — Incidents

Cyber Security: A Look Across Two Decades

Finding 4

Outsourcing and Cloud considerations dominate sharply during a short middle period (2010-11-12) then vanish into acceptance

A sense of Realisation seems to dominate the junction between the 2 decades:

This is no longer JUST about Compliance and Risk: Tech is changing, Threats are real and Incidents do impact Business

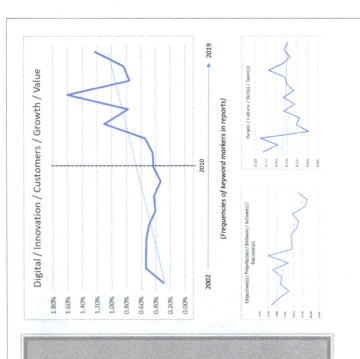

Digital / Innovation / Customers / Growth / Value

(Frequencies of keyword markers in reports)

People / Culture / Skill(s) / Team(s)

Objective(s) / Priority(ies) / Delivery / Action(s) / Decision(s)

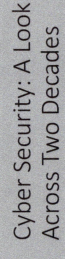

Cyber Security: A Look Across Two Decades

Finding 5

Our Business language tends to sharpen throughout the last decade but our focus on <u>Execution</u> and <u>People</u> tends to dwindle

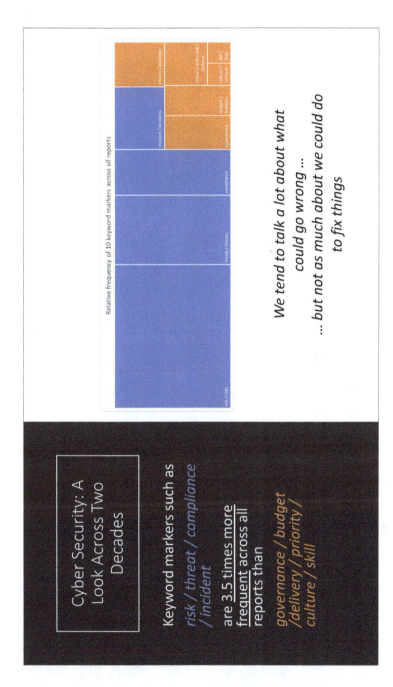

Relative frequency of 10 keyword markers across all reports

Cyber Security: A Look Across Two Decades

Keyword markers such as

risk / threat / compliance / incident

are 3.5 times more <u>frequent across all reports</u> than

governance / budget / delivery / priority / culture / skill

We tend to talk a lot about what could go wrong ...

... but not as much about we could do to fix things

The semantics analysis shows the clear emergence of 2 periods

2002-2009

>> The Compliance Decade

- Security as a balancing act between Compliance Requirements and Risk Appetite (and costs)

The CISO as Risk Manager

2010-2019

>> The Realisation Decade

- Security as a necessary barrier against real Threats in a context of massive technological change (and the aftermath of a historical financial crisis)

The CISO as Fire Fighter

2020 and beyond?

What the next decade must address

2002-2009

>> The CISO as Risk Manager

The Compliance Decade
Security as a balancing act between Compliance Requirements and Risk Appetite (and costs)

2010-2019

>> The CISO as Fire Fighter

The Realisation Decade
Security as a necessary barrier against real Threats in a context of massive technological change (and the aftermath of a historical financial crisis)

Beyond 2020

>> The CISO as Transformation Leader

The Execution Decade
Security as an imperative in the "when-not-if" era, in a context of significant maturity deficit in many firms (and potentially massive regulatory fines)

3 management considerations in conclusion ahead of the next decade

The profile of the transformation leaders will be key

A good "fire-fighter" may not be a good "transformer"

Transformation takes time and there may not be quick-wins

Senior management must be able to look beyond the short-term and stay focused on transformational objectives

More than ever, this is about culture and governance, not just technology

Throwing money at tech vendors will not build anything lasting without the right organisation and operating model

Methodology Summary

We gathered all EY Global Information Security Surveys from 2002 to 2019 in PDF format.

We read each PDF using the pdf_text function from the [pdftools](#) package in order to obtain the full text for each page in machine-readable format. Because of the nature of PDFs, some of the text could not properly be read (fancy headlines, non-standard font in some titles, etc.) but we were successful in getting more than 95% of the content of each report.

We then performed some amount of data cleaning – removing standard English stopwords (e.g. and, but, all, did, ...), all one- and two-letter words, as well as some reports-specific uninformative words such as: ernst, young, annual, survey, percent, or respondents.

We used the [quanteda](#) package – the standard tool for managing and analyzing textual data in R – in order to turn the raw text into analyzable format called a document-feature matrix (dfm).

A dfm is simply a (typically very sparse) matrix where each row i is a different document (here, each row is a year), each column j is a word, and every entry [i, j] is the count of word j in document i. No stemming was performed at this stage.

We computed the top 100 terms for each year and exported the final ranking (along with absolute counts and frequencies) to CSV for easy analysis in Excel. Stemming and grouping of terms was performed manually in Excel using domain-expertise.

After manually selecting the most interesting terms to the analysis, we went back to the dfm to complete the count for those terms in years in which they did not make it to the top 100.

Many thanks to Vincent Viers for his help with the research and the methodology

Index of
Articles

Contents 1

THE
Security
Transformation
RESEARCH FOUNDATION

The Security Transformation Research Foundation supports research projects and individual initiatives aimed at changing the narrative around cyber security, looking beyond the technical horizon into security strategy, governance, culture, and the real dynamics of transformation.

www.securitytransformation.com
Twitter: @Transform_Sec

Corix Partners is a London-based Boutique Management Consultancy Firm, focused on assisting CIOs and other C-level executives in resolving Cyber Security Strategy, Organisation & Governance challenges.

www.corixpartners.com
Twitter: @CorixPartners